VOICES IN YOUR ONSHORE BREEZE

"James MacGregor Burns (1978) states that leadership is one of the most researched, and least understood, topics there is in the world. For decades, I have combed through the research and theory books, and I have never found an approach that provides an exciting and accurate approach to learning leadership — *until now*. While there are many books on leadership, *The Surfer's Journey* is a potentially powerful instructional tool that should be read by all students of leadership.

"Utilizing a great story line, this book draws upon research to provide a unique methodology. It presents a thought-provoking theoretical model, along with practical examples. Dr. Kennedy writes with a wonderful literary style that ultimately delivers an arsenal of tools that may be used in a variety of ways by the audience.

"One strength, and unique characteristic, of this book is that the ideas are not only practical, but are supported by detailed research. In addition to his conducting an extensive literature review, Dr. Kennedy's material is the result of decades of structured observations and data. However, it takes a special style to transform research into a humanistic story filled with adventure, intrigue, and valuable lessons.

"Dale Carnegie wrote that, 'People rarely succeed unless they have fun in what they are doing.' This book is a great example of how learning does not have to be a chore, but can be fun and engaging. In this book, Dr. Kennedy affords the readers a leadership adventure that is well worth the journey."

— Peter M. Jonas, PhD, Professor, Cardinal Stritch University; Senior Partner, Capacity Unlimited; author of *Laughing and Listening: An Alternative to Shut Up and Listen* and *Secrets of Connecting Leadership with Humor*

"From the moment his feet hit the sand until waves finally rushed over his surfboard, I was immersed in *The Surfer's Journey*. The book is enthralling as well as enlightening, leading the novice to become the expert, with surfing as the metaphor for leadership. These are ten principles to live by!"
—Prof. Pamella A. Seay, JD, LLM, Florida Gulf Coast University

"If you own or manage a business, if you are in charge of people, you owe it to them and yourself to go on *The Surfer's Journey*. Dr. Kennedy will lead you on a heroic journey from where you are now — to the leader you know is inside you, the one you catch glimpses of from time to time. You'll be reborn in your fullest capacity, the person your team needs to steer them confidently and profitably into the future while helping each member maximize their personal potential. *The Surfer's Journey* is nothing less than life changing. Heed the ten lessons of he'e nalu. This is one call to adventure you don't want to ignore!"
—Dave Lakhani, CEO, Bold Approach, Inc., Journeyer, Creator, Partner, Father, Mentor, and now, Blissful Surfer! Author of *Persuasion: The Art of Getting What You Want* and *Power of an Hour*

"*The Surfer's Journey* will transport you to a time and place far away, and at the same time put you in touch with your own here and now! Buckle up for a mythical trip of self-discovery and learn essential lessons of leadership that you can put into practice today."
—Nancy Stanford Blair, Professor Emerita, Cardinal Stritch University, Milwaukee, Wisconsin. Author of *Mindful Leadership, Leading Coherently* and *Your Life is Your Message*

"I have been an attorney for thirty-five years. But, first, I was, I am, and I will always be, a Surfer!

"Through surfing, I came to realize that, by keeping yourself committed, focused, and fully engaged in Mind, Body and Soul, you will optimize your success, you will be at peace with all that you do, and, in short, you will be a better you. This is the concept upon which others and I founded The Mind, Body & Soul Surfing Club and MBS Recovery, and this is the concept that my friend and fellow Surfer, Dr. Don Kennedy, builds upon to give you *A Surfer's Journey*.

"Like paddling out when the surf is big and powerful, life can sometimes knock us off track and cause us to dig deeper into who and what we are. This happened to me in 2013 when addiction took my son's life. When life knocks you off track or when you hear that voice in your onshore breeze saying, 'Make a change — have faith,' then you know it's time to build your board and paddle into the unknown. *The Surfer's Journey* will show you the way toward fully engaging your Mind, Body and Soul and finding that better you and that perfect wave of life."

—John W. Foster, Esq., The Orlando Family Firm

"It was my first time in Costa Rica with a group of surfers, most of whom I had never met. The afternoon that we arrived, we immediately went on a surf safari. A few hours later, we found ourselves 100 kilometers away from any civilization, in a new land, and we were about to surf a spot we had never seen.

"After paddling a half-mile out to sea, we approached the surf. It was triple the size that it had looked from the beach. As I reached where the huge swells were exploding on the reef beneath me, each with the sound of semi-tractors slamming into a mountain, a rush came across me.

"I realized that I was halfway across the world, with people whom I did not even know, in the middle of the ocean, miles from civilization, and I could die there that very day and no one could do anything about it. In that moment, a calm rushed across me that I had never experienced before. I trusted this 'gut' feeling, and I paddled directly into the biggest wave of my life.

"I had spent many days thinking of that moment in my life, that 'snapshot,' until I read Dr. Kennedy's book. Much like that rush I received in the ocean that day, this book opened my mind to a better understanding of myself personally and professionally.

"You do not have to be a surfer to 'get it,' but you may be one when you are done. And if so, we will be there for you when you paddle out."

—SCOTT JACKSON, FOUNDER & CEO, JACKSON WORKS, INC.

"I could have really used this book's principles in the beginning when I needed them. As a result of my drug addiction, I had all but quit surfing at the age of twenty-three. I was homeless, I was powerless, and I was hopeless; addiction had taken everything from me. As I began to get my life back together, I waited almost two years to return to the water.

"The principles surfing taught me have been and continue to be the driving force in my recovery life, as well as my business life. Each day and each moment, they are the glue that holds me together. Now, with twenty-eight years clean and twenty-two years of business success, I am grateful to be surfing more than ever. Reading and practicing the ten principles in *The Surfer's Journey* covers all areas of life and business. If you learn and translate them to your everyday life, you can truly accomplish anything."

—LONNY MEAD, PARTNER, THE PRESENTATION GROUP

THE SURFER'S *Journey*

*TO JAKE
AND ALL THE GRANDCHILDREN
WE TEACH*

ALSO BY DR. DON KENNEDY

5 A.M. & Already Behind

Your Smoking Bahbit: 7 Steps to Stop Smoking Now

Lessons from New Smyrna

THE SURFER'S Journey

the path to TRANSFORMATIONAL HEROSHIP

DR. DON KENNEDY
DO | PhD | MBA | CPE | FAAFP

Illustrations by Pamella Seay

Edited by Robin Stonaker

Cover Design by 5 Lakes Design & Think Tank Solutions

Interior Design by 1106 Design

Copyright by Donald Kennedy 2017

All Rights Reserved.

TABLE OF CONTENTS

PART ONE — PADDLE OUT	**1**
Chapter 1 — The Storm	3
Chapter 2 — The Dream	7
Chapter 3 — The Letter	15
Chapter 4 — The Island	23
Chapter 5 — The Story	27
Chapter 6 — The Cove	35
Chapter 7 — The House	43
Chapter 8 — The Journal	49
Chapter 9 — The Myth	57
PART TWO — TRIALS AND PRINCIPLES	**65**
Chapter 10 — The Mentor	67
Chapter 11 — The Ritual	73
Chapter 12 — The Rocks	83
Chapter 13 — The Vision	89
Chapter 14 — The Surfboard	95
Chapter 15 — The Whitewater	103
Chapter 16 — Meeting Evil	111

Chapter 17 — Focus and Crises	119
Chapter 18 — The Volcano	127
Chapter 19 — The Perfect Wave	135
PART THREE — PADDLE IN	**141**
Chapter 20 — The Meeting	143
Chapter 21 — Home	149
Epilogue — Transformational Heroship	163
References	167
Glossary of Terms	175
Creators	181
About Dr. Kennedy	187
It's Time To Paddle Out!	189
What Are You?	191

FOREWORD
Nancy Stanford-Blair, PhD

What I know about surfing could fill a thimble! Boards, wetsuits, and waves are involved, that much I know. What I *do* know about is leadership and transformational change, so when Don brought up the idea of comparing the latter to the former, I was intrigued. Let me explain.

Author Don Kennedy is a wide-eyed, energetic, and curious physician who has been on a lifelong learning quest to expand his cognitive capacity and that of others. With over thirty years of practice, he was frustrated that health care had become so difficult and complex to maneuver and that physicians were in danger of losing their way — their core passion and drive to serve their patients. He was also concerned that the same challenges seemed to be occurring for people in many professions within the fast-changing landscape of the twenty-first century. And he was ultimately concerned that his patients were finding it increasingly difficult to live lives of health and balance.

Several years ago, he decided that his physician's license and his MBA weren't quite enough to find the answers he sought, so he joined a unique doctoral program in Leadership for the Advancement of Learning and Service at Cardinal Stritch

University in Milwaukee, Wisconsin. He entered hungry to learn the most important leadership lessons available and to discover how to share those with others. As his professor, I had many thought-provoking conversations with Don, and this is what I heard:

"I want to write a book," he said.

"I want to engage people in a journey toward their own leadership capabilities, to successfully lead themselves and others," he said.

"I'm a surfer, and I think surfing can be used as a powerful metaphor for teaching these lessons," he said.

"Oh, and I love what you are teaching us about the mythological and structure of the Transformational Hero's Journey, so I want to use that too!" he said.

Really? Leadership, medicine, the Hero's Journey, and surfing? How could that all possibly be related? Leadership is an art and science with a long trail of related research and theory. Medicine is an ancient and very specific and highly skilled field all its own. The Hero's Journey is Joseph Campbell's explanation of the monomyth that describes the path to personal transformation throughout time — from the Bible to *Star Wars*. And surfing? Well, I already told you of my limited knowledge in that category. Only Don could have pulled off the elegant integration of these concepts to teach and inspire personal growth. And pull it off he did.

The doctor, student, and surfer invested five years in the creation of this engaging and delightful tale that will take you on your own Hero's Journey. His resulting narrative creates a transformational path back to wholeness, balance, and well-being — for yourself and others you have the opportunity to influence.

While this book is based on Don's extensive research about effective leadership practice along with the process of transformation change, it is the antithesis of a didactic text with theoretical explanations and never-ending lists of to-dos. Don has found a magical formula to combine powerful, best leadership practices with the tenets of personal transformation and pass them on to you in a mythical and metaphorical *Surfer's Journey*. He describes the book as not a "how to" book, but a "what if" book.

So what if you

... decide right now to begin your own Transformational Hero's Journey?

... determine that you are ready to find the authentic leader within?

... have the courage to look inside yourself and discover the power to do more, be more, feel more?

Sounds pretty amazing, right? How can you possibly say no to the possibilities ahead?

Because of the magnitude of transformational change, I think this book is best read several times. The *first time* through, I recommend you settle in with a warm cup of your favorite beverage — perhaps by the fire or looking out over a vista of your choice — and just enjoy the story. The *next time* through, engage in the opportunities provided to reflect, draw, journal, and wonder about the story line, the characters, and the lessons. And on your *final pass,* you can begin to apply the principles to your own life — your role in your family, your role in your work, your role in your community. And when you have enjoyed every morsel the book has to offer, share or pass it on to someone you care deeply about, so they can discover their own possibilities.

Now are you ready to answer a call to adventure? Are you interested in expanding your influence? Are you willing to invest in yourself? If your answer is yes to any of these questions, then *The Surfer's Journey* is for you! So travel with Don to Hawaii, let your imagination take you along on a thrill ride of adventure, feel the power of the surf, and experience the deep recognition that you can become the hero of your own story — the one you have been waiting for.

—Nancy Stanford-Blair, Professor Emerita, Cardinal Stritch University, Milwaukee, Wisconsin
Author of *Mindful Leadership,*
Leading Coherently and *Your Life is Your Message*

PREFACE

*I*n convention of the fables of mythical heroes, *The Surfer's Journey* is a research- and principle-based mythological tale focused on influencing, instructing, and inspiring the common individual of today to dare answer their call to become a transformational hero, an internal voice ignored by those who accept existence and life as it is.

In the end, *The Surfer's Journey* is a personalized symbolic guidebook for readers, students, educators, and leaders. It melds proven leadership principles with the sport, history, and culture of surfing to move the reader toward the focus and behaviors of a bliss-driven transformational leader and hero: one who is cause-driven, who inspires followers to achieve beyond their present capacity, and whose life purpose is to improve the human condition, despite the sacrifice.

ACKNOWLEDGMENTS

The first principle of *The Surfer's Journey* addresses the need for mentors, those who see what we are before we do. This book is the result of thirty years of learning from the stories and lives of patients, the impact of teachers and surfers, and living and applying the lessons taught by Mother Ocean.

I am grateful for those who encouraged me to answer the voice in my onshore breeze, to paddle out and heal and motivate through my writing, teaching, and speaking. A special thanks to my Cardinal Stritch University mentors, Dr. Peter Jonas and Dr. Nancy Blair, who saw the surfer, the Coydogg, and molded the ideal of leadership and the transformational hero and encouraged me to enter the forest where there was no path. Gratitude to Gulf Coast University professor, attorney, and friend, Pamella Seay, who provided perspective, art, and an example of creative energy and a life of purpose.

There is no existence without love, and my wife and surfer girl, Paula, is the heart of all I do and believe. She has taught me and our family that there are no barriers if you wake each day and just begin.

And finally, thanks to the real-life Kanoa, my best friend, attorney John Foster, for sharing sixty years of dreams, laughs, and the waves.

INTRODUCTION
300 AD

A man stands on a beach boulder on the outermost island of the Marquesas off the coast of Peru. He is godlike, large and thick, and the canary glow of sunset accents his king's physique. Behind him, waves explode on the last reef before the open South Pacific Ocean. An onshore breeze licks the man's herculean back and pushes his long dark hair across his eyes. He wipes his forehead and looks upon the Polynesian tribe sitting in the sand, his followers.

"We must leave this place," the man says.

Their gaze is fixed; they have heard this before.

"Those who would take our freedom are near, and the gods have spoken to me through a dream. I saw an island of mountains, fruit, and pools of fish, a place we can live with our spirits free and where our will cannot be stolen. I saw a permanent home where we can wake and choose, instead of being forced to survive in hiding and fear." He pivots and gestures toward the yellow sky. "It is out there, and in six full moons when the storms have passed, we will leave this shore and find our place of promise."

Those on the beach catch the eyes of others. Some show hope, some fear, and some are closed in prayer. Their king steps from the rock and touches a boy's head.

"We must be prepared for this dangerous journey." The leader looks toward four men, their faces furrowed and weathered.

"You must go to the forest and cut trees to build boats that will take us to this island. Each vessel must hold one hundred people and our goats, birds, seed, and food, and withstand the forces that would destroy our destiny." The man steps toward the craftsmen. "You must begin today and know that the gods and I will smile on your effort, and no matter how many times you fail, you will not be punished. Can you do this?" The four stand and bow, and hope warms the islanders.

The leader points to his guides. "You will pray for fair winds, clear days and nights, and for the gods to send birds to lead us to this new land. Before we leave you must teach others to navigate the stars, as your fathers have taught you." The men lower their chins; their hearts pound with new purpose.

Six months later, the nomads sail double-hulled canoes two thousand miles to an archipelago of islands where they tell stories of heroes and gods, ride waves, and live in blissful isolation for five hundred years and twelve generations. Hawaii.

ABOUT THIS BOOK

This book began as a story I wrote to teach my grandson what I learned from a life of surfing. It began as scribbles on a yellow pad in my home office eight years before I returned to complete my PhD in leadership. But as I pondered my doctoral thesis, the tale and its principles kept popping up; and as I studied Joseph Campbell's works, I realized that surfing, not medicine, was the myth I had lived, and, much like you reading this introduction, a spiritual voice was calling me to begin a journey to teach, speak, and write.

My lessons from surfing began in the sixties on the olive-green spray-painted, cracked and waterlogged Gordon and Smith surfboard I dragged to the water, as my single mother watched from our rusted Rambler parked in the sand on New Smyrna Beach, Florida. She knew that Mother Ocean would teach what she couldn't, and she was right. Fifty years later, the waves of Costa Rica, Hawaii, Florida, El Salvador, and California call, and I pack my board and go to learn more.

This story, *The Surfer's Journey,* is a mythological fable created to teach the principles of leadership, success, and health through the lens and language of surfing. The text combines the tenets of transformational leadership and mythology with the principles gleaned from interviews with surfers who shared a common life theme:

> *No matter the country or life situation — surfing teaches, saves, changes, and improves lives.*

In this book you will be challenged and taught how to begin your own surfer's journey through the actions of a character I call a *transformational hero*, defined as one who is willing to give up all they have and thought was important for a cause greater than themselves; a simple idea, but difficult to do. This is a book about leaving the ordinary life and paddling out to discover what is in your soul that's speaking and pulling you toward a rebirth. I know you hear and feel it.

Today, people blame the endless bombardment of tech-driven information for their overload and anxiety, but that is not the problem. As a geriatric physician for thirty years, I've found that no matter the generation, people tell the same story beginning with *I wish I had* and *if I only*. The problem is that individuals are never taught how to step beyond their self-imposed boundaries to discover what they are and what they could bring to the world. Teaching, mentoring, and motivating people like you to take that one simple action is my life's mission.

About this Book

Now it's your turn. You can act on the voice that is daring you to paddle beyond the horizon where that one wave will give you the thrill of being alive, or stay where you are. It's your choice. I say —

Grab your board and live!

HOW TO MAKE THIS YOUR HE'E JOURNAL

This book is about paddling out, leaving what I call the *island of same,* the ordinary life, learning the principles of surfing, he'e nalu, and ultimately finding and riding your bliss-filled, perfect wave. This is not a *how to* book, it's a *what if* book, and is written as a teaching tool and guidebook for college and professional leadership courses, as well as *The Surfer's Journey* retreats and seminars.

The Surfer's Journey has three parts. **Part One** is preparatory and focuses on the ordinary life, the past and now, and those who hear but ignore the voice in their onshore breeze. **Part Two** represents the daring journey beyond the ordinary life to the subconscious, the shadow, the trials of death, demons, and personal rebirth through the proven ritual of he'e nalu. **Part Three** brings the principles of surfing back to a world that is hungry for their fearless transformational hero, the one who will risk it all for a cause more important than life itself.

The early Hawaiians had no written words; they communicated and taught through mythological stories and symbols for eight hundred years until Captain Cook spoiled the beach party in 1778. I want this book to be unique to you: your thoughts,

The Surfer's Journey

your art, and your creative subconscious voice. So instead of the standard review of the lessons taught, blank pages marked by *The Surfer's Journey* stickman logo have been placed at the end of each chapter to tickle your imagination. ***These pages are for the surfer within you to draw and color and journal.***

THERE ARE NO RULES OR RESTRICTIONS AND NO ONE TO JUDGE, CRITIQUE, OR CRITICIZE.

Whenever you see these blank pages, simply draw or write whatever you are thinking and feeling or what you have learned from that chapter *as shown in the example drawn by a reader on the next page*. Please note that your picture or prose may not come immediately, and it's okay to skip and move on; but be aware that your creative center is awakening and that something in your day or a dream will visit and inspire you to work it out. It's already started. *Please feel free to share your thoughts and images by emailing a picture of your drawing to me at* **don@thesurfersjourney.com**. No names necessary.

What you glean from this book will be unique to this stage of your life's journey, although your first interpretation will surely change. It is my hope that each time you revisit the symbols and art and thoughts you create on the blank pages today, your spirit will be inspired to fight past the urge to stay on the *island of same*. Be daring, experiment, consciously seek new experiences and dare to paddle out while everyone else watches. If you do, I promise you will ride the wave of your life.

How To Make This Your He'e Journal

Example

DR. BLAIR'S RECOMMENDATIONS

1. **The *first time* through,** I recommend you settle in with a warm cup of your favorite beverage — perhaps by the fire or looking out over a vista of your choice — and just enjoy the story.

2. **The *next time* through,** engage in the opportunities provided to reflect, draw, journal, and wonder about the story line, the characters, and the lessons, then begin your journey and learn from the wisdom of the mentor character, Malu, at http://www.drdonkennedy.com/malugrams.

3. **On your *final pass*,** you can begin to apply the principles to your own life — your role in your family, your role in your work, your role in your community.

4. **And when you have enjoyed every morsel** the book has to offer, share or pass it on to someone you care deeply about, so they can discover their own possibilities.

IMPORTANT BEFORE YOU BEGIN: JOURNAL DOWNLOAD

*I*f you are reading from a digital device or PDF or if you want to draw or journal outside this *The Surfer's Journey* book, please download the free Journal PDF at the link below.

http://www.drdonkennedy.com/journal

Please Join Dr. Kennedy's Email List at:
http://www.drdonkennedy.com

PART I
Paddle Out

"The Dark Eye of Evil Blinks"

THE STORM

The only hint of the monster churning three hundred miles from the tiny island is a shift in the evening breeze. By first light, a stiff onshore wind jams whitecaps into the lava shore, skirts the cliff, skims the lawn, and becomes the breath of the baby boy sleeping in the attic bedroom of the plantation house. It is the child's last day on the island.

The gray-haired patriarch turns the radio off then moves to the porch where his wife knits in a creaking swing. He leans over the rail, cocks his head, and follows the counterclockwise flow of the gray clouds.

"The weatherman says the storm will miss us," the woman says without looking up.

"I know, but we can't take that chance. Call Malu and tell him to take the baby to the Big Island and then call Akoni and tell him I'm coming to the office."

Part One: Paddle Out

The creaking stops, and when he hears the rotary phone tick, he pushes from the rail and walks to his green pickup truck. He drives down the hill, travels two miles on a gravel road to a square building, and parks next to a hand painted sign: *Big Kahuna*. He says good morning to the receptionist then opens a smoked glass door labeled *Manager*.

Akoni gazes out the window at the mist-rimmed volcano then swivels to face the man, drums the desk and says, "Are you sure, Father?"

"Yes, son. The seas are rising and there is not enough time to bring a boat. Malu has arranged for a plane to take the boy in one hour, and I've given him written instructions. Your son will be safer there. Notify the staff to tighten down the training center and cottages and use the bus to take the guests to high ground."

Two hundred miles east the barometric pressure drops, and the dark eye of evil blinks.

The Storm

The Storm

THE DREAM

I tossed my shoes on the office floor, propped my legs on the desk, closed one eye, and placed the rising orange ball exactly, exactly, in the V between my crossed feet. That sun is like a new day baby struggling to catch its first breath, but it can't because of the foggy junk blowing from the truck pipes eight stories below. That smut turns lungs black, and I'm supposed to make the wheezers well. I'm tired.

"You had that dream again."

I saw Leah's reflection in the window. She leaned against the door the way she does when she's worried I'm overdoing it. I was.

"It's telling you something, Doc," she said. "People do not have dreams just to have dreams, not like the ones you're having. Maybe you should talk to somebody. How about your friend, Dr. Bane? Maybe you need a vacation."

I scrunched my eyebrows.

Part One: Paddle Out

"Fine. Clinic in an hour," she said. "You've got thirty-five patients, and I'm calling Dr. Bane because I know you won't."

She was right. I pulled my feet to the carpet, picked up the first envelope in a pile of mail, twirled it, put it back, then stuffed all of them in Leah's in-box.

Two days later I knocked then cracked open the door to the psychiatrist's office. "Oh, Dr. Bane, Dr. Bane?" I said in a squeaky voice.

"Well, that must be Dr. John Foster," he said as he stood and, always the joker, clutched his chest. Stew is built like a crane, tall, his face pointed, but he's always friendly and you know you can trust him. He pulled me toward a worn couch.

"Come on, sit down," he said. "I want to hear about this nightmare Leah said you're having." He sunk into a paisley armchair across from me.

"You know I don't want to be here," I said.

"Who does?" he asked. "Don't make this a big deal."

I didn't know how to start. We stared; he knew what I was thinking.

"John, you're not a patient. Let's talk as friends," he said. "I'm not taking notes, look." He flipped his hands. "No pen, no pad, and no recorder."

I cracked my neck, and sucked in two pounds of oxygen.

Chapter 2: The Dream

"So, I'll ask the questions, okay?" he asked. "Let's be half serious."

"I know. I need to figure this out. I haven't slept an eight-hour night in months."

"So let's warm up. When was the first dream?"

"When I was five or six years old," I said. "At first it was colors and little flashes of faces, but now, every night's the same adventure."

"I know you're an orphan, right?"

"Yep, left at an orphanage downtown when I was about six months old and adopted a couple months later."

"And your parents . . . ?"

"I don't know anything about my real parents. My adopted mother died from leukemia when I was twelve, and Ken, my adopted father, died of a heart attack two months after I left for college."

"Was he a good father?"

"My best friend. He was a carpenter, but called himself a furniture artist. He taught me how to work: up early, everything perfection."

"Ever try to find your real parents?"

"Not really," I said. "Ken told me the only record was the address of the orphanage scribbled on a note."

"No name?"

"Nope. Nobody knows where I came from." My voice pitched, but I let it pass and stayed quiet until Stew asked the next question.

Part One: Paddle Out

"Okay, so how did you get here?" he asked. "Medical school? No parents?"

"After Mom died the doctor who took care of her, Dr. Parsons, gave me a few bucks to clean his office after school," I said. "When I was in twelfth grade I was mopping the floor, and he asked me what I was going to do with my life. I said I didn't know. That night I lay in the grass in my backyard watching falling stars and decided I would be like Dr. Parsons. Pretty simple. Funny how people affect your life."

"From there?"

"My father left me the house and insurance money, and I got through college washing dishes and doing carpentry. I plugged along until I was accepted to medical school, and here I am, thirty-four years old. At least I think I'm thirty-four."

"Never married?"

"No, too busy. Never found the right one."

"In practice how long?"

"Five years this month."

"Love it?"

"What?" I heard him; taboo territory.

"Do you like it? Medicine? Being a doctor?"

"Tough question. Yes and no," I said. "I love taking care of patients, they're my friends. But papers and computers suck the life out of it. I guess the scale is tipped toward no, and the yes is in the kid watching the stars."

"And the dream?" he asked.

Chapter 2: The Dream

My gut dropped. "Ah, the dream. It's weird, so don't think I'm crazy."

"Just talk, John."

"Okay, here goes," I said. "You know I've never told this to anyone?"

"I understand."

I stared at a swirl on Stew's chair. "I'm standing on a beach somewhere, looking at a cove of thick aqua that's beating like a heart. I look down and my toes are sticking out of what look like pearls, except they're wet, and their wiggling." I pulled myself deeper.

"There's somebody next to me, a huge bare-chested guy, he's grinning but he has not eyes. He wraps his arm around my neck and points toward the water.

"I look and see a full moon touching the horizon, and the sky is orange. Then these ten white rays explode out of the moon and start tapping on the ocean like it's a piano. Everywhere the beams touch, a V-shaped wave pops up. There's fifty, then a hundred, and they're marching toward me; and when they hit the beach they explode into silver glitter and soak into the pearls around my feet." I stopped and opened my eyes and looked at Stew, but that's not who I saw.

"Then the muscular guy runs down the beach and jumps and squats on a silver wing he yanks out of the beams and starts carving it around the sky. I'm watching him get farther and smaller, then he turns into this huge white bird and flaps away into the moon.

Part One: Paddle Out

"He's gone. I feel so, so, hollow. I start crying. I want him to come back. I try to yell but can't open my mouth. Then it starts raining and the drops sting, and I try to run but can't pick up my legs. I look down and black snakes are coiled around my ankles, and they're pulling me into the pearls. It's quicksand. It's up to my chest, then my throat. I'm suffocating. I scream then there's a flash, then it's dark."

"John, come out of it. Come on, take your time."

Stew was next to me.

"Are you all right?" he asked.

"Yeah, I think so. That's never happened before. Um."

"Let's take a break."

The Dream

The Dream

3
THE LETTER

"I didn't know you owned land," Leah said.

"What?"

"Read this. It's from a Ben Graham, an attorney in Los Angeles. He says he represents a development company that's interested in land they say you own in the Pacific, but they don't give specifics."

"Let me see that."

The letterhead was embossed gold: *Graham, Crowell, Coy and Mead, Attorneys at Law.*

"Do you think it's a hoax?" she asked.

"Yep," I said. "But we'd better check it out. Try to set up a conference call with Mr. Graham tomorrow. Hang up if it smells fishy."

Leah left and I stood at the window and watched the people and traffic. Stew had warned me that the dream represented something that was trying to break out of my subconscious, and now every emotion that didn't fit my world triggered a sweat alarm.

Graham passed Leah's sniff test. We connected the next day.

"Mr. Graham," I said.

"Dr. Foster, you're a hard guy to find."

"I didn't know I needed to be found. What's this about, Counselor?" I asked.

"Well, I can't tell you a lot more right now. The reason I wanted to talk was to set up a meeting with you and some executives in a couple weeks."

"So, this letter about the property in the Pacific is for real?"

"Absolutely. We've searched historical documents for two years."

"Any doubt?"

"Let's say that what we've found indicates there's a relationship between an island and you. I'll show you what we have at the meeting."

"What if I met with you first?" I asked.

"I'm sure they'll be fine with that," he said. "Let me know the dates, and we'll get you a flight."

"I'll have my secretary call your office."

"Okay, I'll see you in Santa Monica."

This is nuts, I thought.

I slept in first class, and when I arrived at the Los Angeles baggage claim, a driver wearing a black tux was holding my suitcase.

Chapter 3: The Letter

"Dr. Foster?" he asked.

"Yes." How odd. "How did you know that was my bag?"

"I've been coming to this airport for twenty-five years," he said. "Plus," he winked, "your name is on the tag." I followed him to a white limo, and forty minutes later we parked at the Terrace Café in Venice Beach.

"Here we are," he said.

"I thought I was meeting Mr. Graham at his office."

"He wishes this was his office."

Good sense of humor. The door opened and a tanned beach boy leaned in.

"Welcome to California, Doctor Foster," he said "I'm Ben Graham."

"You're kidding."

"Nope," he said. We shook, and I stepped into his world.

"I'm overdressed," I said.

"Nah, what we wear here doesn't define who we are," he said. "I did the big city coats and sleeves and ties; not for me."

I noticed a tattoo on Ben's shoulder as he passed a hundred dollar bill to the driver.

"Family okay?" he asked.

"Yes sir, Mr. Graham."

Ben turned to me and said, "Ed will take your bag to your room. It's on the beach two blocks from here. The idea is to enjoy this, right?"

I nodded; too much happiness.

"You hungry?" Ben asked.

Part One: Paddle Out

"Starved."

"We'll eat, then talk. Okay with you?"

"Perfect," I said. It really was.

We sat in a private room on the second floor in the nook of a bay window that overlooked the Venice pier.

"I'm in the wrong business," I said. Ben's face had crow's feet; he's thirty-five, maybe thirty-eight.

"Yeah, I thought the same way about practicing law in New York until I visited my uncle who's an attorney here. I was blaming the wrong thing. Do I look unhappy?"

We small-talked and ate ahi tuna and seaweed salad. Ben had two children, loved paddle boarding, and by dessert I knew he was authentic. He cared about people and what he was doing, but I kept my guard up just in case.

"Dr. Foster," he said.

"John."

"That's even better. Let's get to business."

"Sounds good."

"This isn't complicated," he said. "I represent a company, but my purpose is to help both of you. I have no special interest in the outcome. My job is to coordinate and make sure you and the executives have the information necessary to make quality decisions. They agreed it was a good idea for you and I to go over the facts. Ready?"

"Go for it."

"Two years ago we received a call from the CEO of Kuanset Corporation, Cecil Stone. Kuanset is a global company that

Chapter 3: The Letter

renovates historic properties into high-class vacation and business destinations."

He opened a brochure and pointed to the picture of a castle on a hill overlooking a village.

"Here's an example of what they do," Ben said. "No one except the family heirs had lived in this castle in rural England for eight centuries. Kuanset bought the property and took it from crumbling to a profitable twelve-room getaway. The customers come for the quiet and the history, and the town merchants make money on the tourism."

I flipped through the brochure. "What does this have to do with me?" I asked.

"Mr. Stone told us they were interested in an island off the coast of the Big Island of Hawaii. A hurricane destroyed a resort there three decades ago. The company couldn't locate the owners and the islanders wouldn't talk, so they hired us and — ta-da — we found you."

"I own an old resort?"

"There's a little more to it. John, we discovered your great-great-grandfather was deeded that island in a land parcel grant in the mid-1800s."

"Are you sure you have the right person?" I asked.

"We tracked you to that orphanage from handwritten instructions we found in the archives. Trust me, according to the dates and a handwriting match of those instructions, you're the only living relative to that family line, so you indeed are the proud owner of the island of . . . Tronahu." He slapped the table.

Part One: Paddle Out

There was a flash of that dream day in Stew's office.

"Hey, drink some water." He handed me a glass.

I swallowed, then wiped my forehead with a napkin. "I'm all right."

"Can I ask you a question?"

"Shoot."

"Do you know anything about your family?"

"No, you're the only one who knows my real name." Ben didn't bite.

"That explains it."

"What do I do now?"

"Think a minute, what do you want to do?"

I sat back and watched the people on the pier. ""Okay. Okay. I want to see Tronahu." Where did that come from?

"Well, why not?" Ben said. "I'll call Mr. Stone and tell him we'll meet when you get back. Hey, it's your island."

"It's my island."

"It is your island." We laughed.

The Letter

The Letter

THE ISLAND

I flew back and called Stew. I told him about the meeting and that I didn't care about selling the island, but that I just wanted my name. A week later, I was sitting in a Kuanset-logoed helicopter on the island of Hawaii watching a scruffy-faced pilot named Joe tug my seat belt.

"Not too tight?" he asked.

"No, that's good."

"Ever been in a chopper?"

"No."

"Put this headset on," he said. "I'll go over the instructions. The most important thing is that paper bag."

I looked down. "Great."

"It's not bad," he said. "We'll fly low so you can see the waves. It's not far, half an hour. Ready?"

Part One: Paddle Out

Ten minutes later we thumped two hundred feet above blue rollers. I kept thinking I could die if we crashed, but probably wouldn't.

"There it is," Joe said. He pointed to a green speck. "It's shaped like a thumb. The north end is a dead volcano; we'll go around that and come in from the east."

He eased the stick back and we climbed.

"See those clouds and that peak?" he asked. "That's the crater. It's an ecosystem. Constant rain up there; that's where the island gets its water. Everything depends on that."

We rounded the volcano, shot over the ocean, dipped and turned, then crossed the shoreline.

"See those green patches?" he asked. "Pineapples and cane."

A postcard.

"Hang on."

I saw an orange windsock flapping over a circular zone cut in a field. A pickup truck was parked on the perimeter. The chopper hovered then bumped down inside a wall of sugarcane stalks.

"I'm gonna keep this running, Doc. Hop out and grab your gear."

Gear, I love pilot talk. I threw off the harness, jumped to the ground, snatched my bag, then ran, crouched, and gave a thumbs-up. Cool. The pilot waved two fingers to remind me he would be back in two days, and then he was gone. I was in Jurassic Park.

"Welcome to Tronahu, Doctor Foster."

The Island

THE STORY

A small man approached me. His face was a smiling raisin, and he squinted in the shade of a straw cowboy hat.

"I am Malu," he said. "We have been waiting for you."

"We?" I asked.

"My wife and I. You will be staying in our guest house."

"I appreciate that," I said.

"Come, I will take you to your room, then show you the island."

A path cut through the sugarcane opened into a tilled black field. Malu tossed my suitcase into the bed of his truck and motioned for me to get in. I stood with my hand on the door. "Well, here I am."

We drove in ruts that split two fields dotted with green shoots, then turned onto a gravel road.

Part One: Paddle Out

"How long have you been on the island?" I asked.

"I was born here sixty-four years ago."

"So you know why I'm here?"

"I do," he said. "I have spoken to the men who wish to buy the island."

"So you were here when the storm hit." I knew I was being abrupt.

"Yes," he said. He flinched but kept smiling.

Twenty minutes later we turned into a drive in front of two white-framed houses engulfed in palms and flowers.

"Come, meet my wife," Malu said.

A woman in a yellow muumuu bounced from the doorway of the first house. She stood on her tiptoes and placed a lei of purple orchids around my neck. Her dark hair was short with streaks of gray, her smile was contagious, and her eyes were different colors: blue and brown.

"Welcome, Doctor," she said as she curtsied.

"This is my wife, Kiana," Malu said. "She will be taking care of you."

"Thank you, Kiana. These are beautiful."

"In Hawaii, our home is your home."

"Were you born here, too?"

"Of course" she said. "Now come with us, I have prepared lunch at the guest house."

We crunched fifty yards down a shell path and through an open-air tin-roofed house to a bamboo table under a gardenia tree.

Chapter 5: The Story

"A Hawaiian lunch for you," Kiana said as she uncovered a plate. "This is pineapple, this is papaya, and I thought you would like to try poi. Also, we left some things in the bedroom for you."

"This is wonderful, Kiana."

Malu appeared. "Your bags are on the bed. Please eat and I'll pick you up in two hours, if that's okay."

"Yes, of course." So this was what freedom felt like.

After the meal I found shorts, sandals, and a flowered shirt in the bedroom closet, then dozed in a cross breeze. Malu knocked three hours later.

"How was lunch?" he asked.

"Perfect, Malu."

"Are you ready to see our paradise?"

"You bet," I said. "Do I need to bring anything?"

"Sunglasses." So simple.

We left Malu's and bumped south toward the coastline.

"Where are we going?" I asked.

"To a place to tell a story."

"What kind of story?"

"Hold on." Malu yanked right and we climbed a road clogged by huge ferns to an ocean cliff.

"Follow me," he said. "Be careful, it's slippery."

We walked to a ledge leaning over a coral head blasted with breaking waves that made me think of the way lions sneak in on their prey and pounce and roar.

"Look there," Malu said. He pointed to a cove that disappeared around the coast.

"It's breathtaking."

"It's more than that," Malu paused. "Doctor, this was your grandfather's quiet place."

What did he say? "You knew my grandfather?"

"Yes."

"My mother and father?"

"Yes. I worked for your family."

"So is this the story?"

"There is more," he said. "The people living on Tronahu are the children of those who discovered Hawaii a thousand years ago." He pointed. "Can you see the mouth of the cove?"

I saw an opening to the ocean in the center of a rocky black line that walled the outer bay.

"That is where the Tronahu natives fought for freedom, led by kings who followed their Polynesian tradition. Doctor Foster, you must understand, within you runs the last blood of those kings."

I heard him, but it didn't soak in deep enough to register an emotion before he pointed toward the cove again.

"The gods burned a symbol in a rock where the beach meets the cliffs. That is the sacred place where families worshiped and gained divine strength call *mana*. People still believe that the spirits of the gods and kings living in that cove protect their way of life from the outside world."

Now I understood why no one spoke to Kuanset.

Chapter 5: The Story

"When the farming industry became difficult," he said, "Tronahu elders looked for other ways to support their families. It was your grandfather's hand that led that change. He built a resort style school near the cove, a place for lost souls to re-think their lives, to begin a *huaka'i* — a new journey. People, from executives to priests, came to learn the secrets your grandfather taught."

"Secrets?" I asked.

"The principles of your ancestors, truths not known beyond Tronahu."

I couldn't hold back. "Why don't I know this, Malu? Why didn't anyone find me or tell me about this place? How did I end up in an orphanage? What happened to my mother?"

"I'm sorry," he said. "Your mother passed when you were born, and your grandmother cared for you while your grandfather and father worked. Then the storm struck."

"The hurricane." I backed off.

"It hit Tronahu on February eleventh, thirty-four years ago," he said. "Your grandfather saved many people, but your father and grandparents died in the tsunami that swallowed the coast. It was a sad time."

"But Malu, how am I here?" I asked.

"The better question, Doctor, is not how you are here, but why you are here."

"No, Malu," I said. "How did I survive?"

"Your grandfather sensed the storm," he said. "Kiana and I flew you to the Big Island after I received a call from your grandmother. We left you and your grandfather's instructions with friends that ran an orphanage."

"You saved my life?"

Malu sighed. "We saved you, but lost you. The same storm struck the Big Island and killed your grandfather's friends. We believe that in the confusion to save the children, you were mixed with orphans sent to the States."

I didn't know what to say. In its absurdity it made sense.

"Enough talk for today," Malu said. "Rest, and tomorrow I will take you to the cove."

The Story

The Story

THE COVE

Before bed I sat on the steps and called Leah.

"How's it going, Dr. Hawaii?" she asked.

"You wouldn't believe it if I told you."

"Let me guess; you need more time."

"Bingo. Maybe a week or so."

"I already blocked your schedule for two weeks."

"Okay. I'll let you know if anything changes."

"Don't worry, I've got everything covered. Just have fun."

I imagined Malu returning to devastation; losing his friends and family. I had a zillion questions but knew the old Hawaiian would reveal the answers in his own way. I slept eight hours without dreaming, and the next morning lay on the couch and read *Atlas Shrugged* until Kiana knocked.

Part One: Paddle Out

"Good morning, Doctor," she sang, "I have breakfast." She placed a plate of scrambled eggs and sliced pineapple on the kitchen table.

"I see you found the coffee," she said.

"I did. This is terrific, better than home."

"Did you sleep well?"

"The best in years." That was the truth.

"That's because you are here. We work hard doing what we love; the nights belong to the gods," she said as she backed toward the door. "Malu will be here in a little while. He is checking the fields. Please let me know if you need anything."

"I will." I wanted to ask Kiana if she knew my mother but kept the question for later.

Malu arrived and we drove several miles into a town located at the end of the pineapple fields.

"This is Ohana," Malu said. "No skyscrapers, but we have a grocery and laundry and the Ohana Café."

"*Ohana?*" I asked.

"It means family. It is where the island was settled." Malu honked at a worker wearing rubber boots who waved without looking then ducked into a shed.

"One of our foremen," Malu said. "The people farm and fish much the way their ancestors did. They still rely on the island for what they have and eat."

Twenty minutes later the road became bumpy and lined with palm trees.

Chapter 6: The Cove

"See how the palms on either side are perfectly spaced?" Malu asked. "Your grandfather planted those. The tsunami drowned this area, and they were the only survivors. I haven't been here in a long time."

I stayed quiet.

"Since the storm, the families moved higher to be safe. Now look," he said.

The pickup slowed, and Malu held the steering wheel with his knees and talked with his hands.

"See how the palms gradually get closer to each other? Your grandfather wanted them to be the fingers of the spirits closing and holding the students."

The road ended and we parked in a half circle of weed-covered shale.

"This was the entrance to the resort. We will walk from here."

The path was dark under a dense canopy, and we stepped over the bodies of broken trees matted with vines, then stopped in a box-shaped clearing.

"Here was the guest check-in, and ahead, spread toward the cove, were cottages," he said. "Each was quiet and private with a path that led to the beach and teaching center."

"Teaching center?" I asked.

"Yes. Remember, the people came to learn the lessons your grandfather taught."

"These were the secrets you were talking about?"

"Yes." Malu chose his words. "Your grandfather taught the ancient principles of *heʻe nalu*," he said.

Part One: Paddle Out

"He'e?"

"He'e means surfing."

Now something was happening: the dream, a link.

"Doctor, life on Tronahu was governed by the principles and rituals of he'e nalu, the sport of the gods. Everyone rode waves — kings, priests, and the common people — and it was expected as proof of their belief. The laws were passed to the generations through stories of kings and heroes killing monsters and riding impossible waves long before the written word. The punishment for breaking the laws of he'e was death."

"And he taught those?"

"Yes, but he reinterpreted them for today's culture to help the students find what he called their perfect wave of bliss. Follow me."

We walked down a narrow path splashed with sunlight darts. The pounding of waves became louder as the trail eased from pebbles to sand, then ended as we stepped into a glaring day.

"Whoa." I didn't expect this one. The cove was the nightmare: a black sand beach cradling aqua pools surrounded by sheer shrub-pocked cliffs. Waves peeled left and right. I closed my eyes and layered the dream over the picture before me and let my imagination play out the fantasy in fast-forward.

Malu removed his sandals and walked to the water.

"You haven't told me everything, have you?" I asked, "Malu."

I knew he heard me, but he didn't answer, so I waited.

"Come with me," Malu said. We walked a half-mile and stopped at the tip of a flat peninsula that jutted into the cove.

"Here, see?" Malu asked.

Chapter 6: The Cove

I looked down and saw an etching of a stickman on a surfboard chiseled into the rock. Its knees were bent, and its outstretched arms held the sun in one palm and the moon in the other. Above the symbol were ten stars filled with saltwater that reflected the sky.

"What does this mean?" I asked.

"*Ku'oko'a*. Freedom. Freedom to live the life of he'e," Malu said. "Remember, this is the holy place where the islanders placed gifts and received mana. All the people of Tronahu carry this symbol in one form or another. No one comes here now."

"Why not?"

"It is forbidden."

"Because of the storm?"

"Yes."

So that was why the cove was empty.

"Doctor, I know this may be confusing," Malu said.

"Confusing?"

"Now we will drive to a special place."

"I thought this was the special place?"

"Your grandfather's home."

"You said everything was destroyed in the storm."

Malu held up one finger as he pivoted. "I said the cottages and the school were destroyed."

The Cove

THE HOUSE

Halfway back to town, we turned between two palms and climbed above a canopy of veined fronds. We stopped on a mesa overlooking the wall of coral protecting the cove.

"We're here," Malu said.

In the center of the mesa was a two-story house wrapped in brown vines facing a lawn that sloped to a cliff. The porch was sagging, and the windows were cross-boarded. I'd been here before; another piece to the puzzle.

"Your grandfather and grandmother built this house for that view. You were born in that room," Malu said as he pointed to a single attic window below the peaked roof. "That is where your grandmother rocked you every morning. She believed the sunrise fed your spirit."

"So my entire family lived here?" I asked.

Part One: Paddle Out

"Yes. The islanders believe their spirits are still here, so they keep it clean, but no one has entered the house since the storm."

We walked to the steps; the wood on the house was gray, like old bones. Two rusted hooks hung from the porch crossbeam.

"So here is where I started," I said.

"Yes. But let me show you something else," Malu said.

I followed the bent Hawaiian to the front of a detached barn-like building padlocked by a chain running through the handles of two wooden doors.

"What's in here?" I asked.

"We are not sure. This was your grandfather's workshop; he locked it the day of the storm."

I walked around the side and tried to peek through the cracks of the boarded windows, but couldn't see anything.

"Would you like to go in the house?" Malu asked.

"I don't know." I thought for a minute and felt the weight of the day. "Nah, I've had enough."

I kept to myself on the way to Malu's, but the words *answerless solitude* kept popping into my mind, and I had no clue what that meant. I was missing something.

"Kiana and I will be traveling to the Big Island for two days," Malu said as we pulled into his driveway. "Use the truck, we will take my brother's van to the boat."

He handed me the keys.

"I will leave a map on the seat. Your meals are set up with my friend, Kala, at the Ohana Café. It opens at six and serves until everyone leaves."

Chapter 7: The House

"Thanks for what you're doing," I said.

"No problem. It would be good to have time to yourself. It is a magic island. Try to meet the people, they know you are here."

"Who's 'they'?"

Malu grinned. "There are no secrets on Tronahu, Doctor. And besides, it is your island."

I'd heard that before.

The House

The House

8

THE JOURNAL

That night the dream changed. The man pulled the silver wing from the moonbeam, pointed to the cliff below the old house, and then zipped through the sky. But this time the white bird turned back, and suddenly I was hugging a feathered neck and the wind was pushing my face. We glided inches above the waves, then swooped up the cliff and dove through an almond mist toward my grandfather's home. I saw two women standing on the lawn next to a baby carriage; they waved then faded just as the bird dropped me in that exact spot.

The house was new, bright white, and the big man was standing on the porch gesturing toward the workshop. Then I was at the workshop door watching my hand trying to touch the padlock, but it kept squirming, and then it raised and slammed into the door: BAM. Then faster like gunshots: BANG, BANG, BANG.

Part One: Paddle Out

I jolted up in bed and stared into the dark. A downpour pounded the tin roof, and the wind slammed a branch into the closed shutters. I laid back and watched the fan blades stutter in the lightning, then checked the time: four a.m. "Man!"

I closed my eyes and relived the dream, and something tapped my subconsciousness.

"That's it, that's it, that's it," I said. I dressed, grabbed the keys, drove through puddles past a pale light in the Ohana Café, and searched for the turn to the house.

"There it is."

I whipped the truck between the palms, parked on the mesa facing a blond horizon, and marched to the place where I had seen the women. I faced the house and threw out my arms.

"Okay, I'm here. I am here." Quiet. Louder. "Hey, I know you hear me."

A glimmer struck the peak above my bedroom window. Then I saw it.

The shimmering outline of the large man floated from the porch toward the workshop. If I was supposed be scared, I wasn't.

"Grandfather?" No answer.

I took slow steps, but before I reached the building, I heard a *clink*, then the ghost faded through the closed doors. So there

Chapter 8: The Journal

I was, by myself in a pastel morning staring at an open lock and a dangling chain.

"What have I gotten myself into?" I knew leaving wasn't an option and that I was acting on an instinct instead of the logic that would have normally stopped me, but it didn't matter.

I gripped the handle and tugged, but the door was stuck in the grass, so I dug it out and yanked it open far enough to slip inside.

The air was heavy, musky, and light strained through the boarded and caked windows. I saw tall forms lining the walls. I exhaled, "Surfboards."

I waited until my eyes focused and could make out the shape of a worktable at the back of the shop. I took two steps. Suddenly a sunlight laser squirted through a hole in the front wall, crept along the floor and stopped on a brass key protruding from a wooden box on the center of the table.

"Okay — I get it." I wasn't alone.

I eased to the table, turned the key, opened the top and saw a leather journal with the stickman symbol and the words *Ku'oko'a 'Uhane* burned into the cover. A folded envelope was next to the book, so I slid it out and held it in the light. The word *Grandson* was scribbled on the back, so I opened it.

Part One: Paddle Out

Dear Grandson,

Before you are the ten sacred principles passed to the kings of each generation. These are the lessons sent by the gods to guide the spiritual lives and ensure the triumph of your ancestors who protected Tronahu.

Grandson, you are reading this letter and are brought to this light by powers beyond those you can understand at this moment. You must trust my words as written and know that the future, your future, and the lives of the many people you touch will be the fulfillment of a prophecy that existed long before you were born. Live, trust, and teach the principles before you today. It is your calling and your destiny.

Grandfather

Chapter 8: The Journal

"*Ku'oko'a 'Uhane* means free spirit." A voice behind me.

I jumped and dropped the paper. A silhouette blocked the doorway.

"Malu," I said. "Man, I thought you left the island."

"I did, but I was called back."

"For this, right?"

"The book has been waiting a long time," he said. "It belongs to you and the people of Tronahu. It is best to leave it here until we talk."

I picked up the note and locked it in the box with the journal, just as I'd found it.

"Kanoa," Malu said.

"What?"

"Your name is Kanoa. It means *the free one*."

"Kanoa. So that's who I am."

"Come, we will go to breakfast. I know you have questions."

"Yeah, that's a good idea."

THE MYTH

Twenty minutes later I was sitting in a booth next to a window at the Ohana Café watching workers load a truck with water cans.

"Aloha, Malu. Who do we have here?"

Malu cleared his throat. "This is John, John Kanoa."

That name.

"John, this is Kala," Malu said.

I turned. Kala was a goddess, her eyes pool-blue over carved cheeks, and her skin a smooth light chocolate. A white flower was tucked behind her right ear, and a braid of shiny black flowed to a knot that touched the shoulder of her uniform. My face burned and I made a noise, but it wasn't a word.

"We have a tradition on the island when we meet someone," she said as she closed the flower in my palm. "There, now we are officially friends."

Part One: Paddle Out

I pulled myself to awareness. "Thank you. I mean, *mahalo*."

"Kala is our island everything," Malu said. "She feeds us, is our nurse, and she works the fields."

"How did you get to the island?" I asked. Stupid question.

"I was born here just like my parents, but I left for a while."

"To where?"

"I studied business and nursing in Los Angeles, then came home," she said. "This restaurant, or something like it, has been here for hundreds of years. My family owns it and I run it."

"You didn't stay in the States?" I was struggling.

"I think it's time for coffee." She patted my arm and sideglanced at Malu.

"John," I said.

"John Kanoa," she said, then spun and whipped through the kitchen doors.

I leaned in. "Okay, Malu, what's this all about?" He arched his eyebrows and looked out the window.

"Malu, sooner or later I've got to get back to my real life. What's in my grandfather's journal?"

"It is easier to tell you the story of Kanoa," he said.

I waited.

"Within your grandfather's journal are the principles and rituals that guided life on Tronahu. They come from a Hawaiian fable told a million times over a thousand years."

I waited.

Malu scooted forward and spread his fingers like blooms.

Chapter 9: The Myth

"Kanoa was the future king of Tronahu and in love with Princess Kailani," he began. "She was chosen as Kanoa's wife in a meeting of the protector god Kane with the spirits of the sun and the moon."

"One day, while Kane was sleeping, the evil squid serpent Kanaloa transformed itself into a handsome prince and sailed into the cove in a golden vessel. The monster knew if it won the heart of Princess Kailani, it would become more powerful than Kane and control the oceans and Tronahu.

"Kanaloa lied to the villagers: 'I am Kane,' it said, 'I am the god of the ocean and sun and moon,' and the islanders welcomed the false god with a seven-day feast. But when Kailani refused Kanaloa, stating her love for her prince, the creature told the islanders, 'I will bring you abundance by kissing the right hand of your princess.' Then as it pressed its lips to Kailani's palm, it transformed itself into the squid, inhaled Kailani's spirit, and hid it in the dark caves deep beneath the reef beyond the cove. Then Kanaloa thrashed its tail and created storms and giant waves and prevented the islanders from leaving to fish and feed their families.

"When Kanoa saw Kailani fall, he held her body and wept, then stopped eating and went to a cave above the cove to die. He grew weaker each day, and each night he dreamed of saving his princess. When the gods of the sun and the moon saw the dreams, they called upon Kane, who lit the cave with fire and spoke to Kanoa: 'To rescue Kailani's spirit,' he said, 'you must prove yourself worthy to be king of the people.'"

Malu froze; a punctuation. He held up three fingers.

"Then Kane gave Kanoa three things: a bag containing ten magic stones broken from the tips of stars, a giant white feather plucked from his soul, and a blazing lava knife. 'Within these stones lies the wisdom of he'e nalu,' he told Kanoa. 'Throw each to the ocean god, and you will be given the wisdom and resolve to survive the challenges Kanaloa will send to crush your willpower.

"'Once you have survived the trials, you must ride the feather through the heart of the great wave beyond the cove and dive to the gates of lost souls. There you must battle Kanaloa and sever its tail with the lava knife to stop the monster's storms of hate. If you succeed, the gates will open and you will find Kailani's spirit.'"

Malu stopped.

"Is that it?" I asked.

"The story is longer, told over many nights."

"So, I guess he did it. Saved the princess?"

Malu shrugged and grinned.

"And that's what's in the journal."

"Not only the lessons of he'e nalu, Doctor, but the sacred ritual taken by young men and kings to prove their manhood."

"They went through an actual ritual?"

"Yes, just like Kanoa in the story, they proved themselves by riding the giant waves that break on the reef outside the cove." Malu paused. "The people still believe the story."

"Still?" I thought for a minute. "The storm."

"Kanaloa came back." Silence. "The people are waiting."

Chapter 9: The Myth

"Waiting?"

"For their king."

That caught me off guard. "Wait a minute, that's not me, Malu. That's crazy."

"Believe what you want, Doctor. Either way, it will be you that decides the future of Tronahu." He sat back.

"Listen — Malu." I'd forgotten what pressure felt like. "I think I need to get back to the real world for a while. I need time to think. You understand, right?"

"Of course. I will call for a helicopter."

"What about the journal?"

"It must stay on the island."

Two hours later I pressed my nose against the bubble of the chopper and waved to Malu who was leaning against his pickup. Something didn't fit. This wasn't medicine: there were no guidelines, no rules, and no orders. I kept telling myself I had to leave, but there was a gnawing I couldn't suppress with my doctor common sense. As the shadow of the Mauna Loa volcano appeared over the Big Island, something snapped.

"There's just no quick fix for this one." I pulled the pilot's sleeve and gestured a circle.

"What?" he asked.

"Turn around. We've got to go back, I forgot something." He shrugged, tilted the stick, and cut a U in the cloudless sky.

As we approached the landing zone I saw the old Hawaiian hadn't moved, and for the first time, I knew something else was in control of my life. I decided to let it happen.

"How did you know?" I asked as I walked to Malu.
"I didn't, but you did."
"What now?"
"You must become a man."
"I am a man."
"You must follow the ritual."
"What will I have to do?"
Malu's eyes laughed. "You will learn that tomorrow."

The Myth

PART TWO
Trials and Principles

"You Must Follow the Ritual"

THE MENTOR

Kiana drove me to the old resort at sunset the next day. As I reached for the handle, she pressed her fingers on my wrist, chanted under her breath, then smiled and said, "Take the left path to the end of the cove, then turn and follow the shore to the fire. Pomaika'i. Good luck, Kanoa."

I did as Kiana said and walked along the shore with my sandals in a backpack Malu had given me. Halfway around the cove the afterglow turned the water tangerine orange, so I waded in and splashed it on my face and arms. I thought the water felt odd, silky, but didn't understand what had happened until I walked onto the beach; *my shadow was gone.*

"So, this is how it begins."

I continued toward a thread of smoke until I saw Malu sitting on a log next to a fire built in the sand between the stickman symbol and a sheer rock face. A yellow-feathered cloak was

Part Two: Trials and Principles

draped around his shoulders, flowers hung across his chest, and his face was painted with yellow, blue, and red lines.

"Aloha, Kanoa," he said.

"Aloha, Malu." What happened to doctor?

"Please, sit."

I sat cross-legged on the other side of the fire, then Malu walked over, placed the lei around my neck, and returned to the log.

"The forces that pulled you here," he said, "are not definable in the world you have lived. You have crossed a threshold into the unknown and today you begin the journey of your ancestors. Although I will guide you, the journey is yours. The gods will choose their own means of helping in your transformation."

Transformation. The word had a kick.

"Kanoa, the principles you will learn are powerful and will guide the decisions of your life," he said. "You will have proven your manhood when you have ridden the great wave beyond the cove. Only then will this journey end and a new one begin. We will meet here each sunrise and follow the ritual of he'e nalu, just as your ancestors did before the great storm. Your challenges will be great, and dark spirits will test your resolve."

I thought a second. "Why are you doing this Malu? I mean, why you?"

"I am called. I am your mentor."

That answer was too short.

"Kanoa, you cannot go on this journey alone. Just like I am here, there have always been helpers in your life."

Chapter 10: The Mentor

I thought about my adopted father, then it hit me. "Was Ken real?"

"All your teachers are real, Kanoa. There is one difference." He paused.

"They have already found and ridden their great wave, their perfect wave. You can see it in see the spark of wisdom in their eyes and hear it in their laughs as they carve their names on each wave. They are fearless, Kanoa, they are the models of surfing freedom, and they live each day to teach and serve through the ten principles of he'e nalu. You ask if they are real, your grandfather would answer by saying, 'they knew the king within you long before you did. Now it is your turn to discover the seed of purpose waiting in the shadow of your soul.'"

Malu walked over, extended his hand, and pulled me within an inch of his nose.

"You ask why I am here? I am here to carry you beyond the threshold of the meaningless. I am here to guide you through the physical and mental trials the common man sees as too dangerous, too impossible, and too risk-laden. I am here because I have been called to impart the rituals of the gods and to listen, encourage, and push you beyond the shore where, as your grandfather would say, 'many wade to their ankles then stop in empty fear and return to their *beach of same* and babble in false satisfaction.'"

He dropped my hand. His voice was low and edged. "You must know that I will not let you fail, Kanoa, just as the leader in you must never stop mentoring those islanders and students who will one day sit here and stare at the ocean and wonder if they are worthy."

I puffed out my cheeks, looked at my feet, and tried to say something profound but all that came out was, "How long will this take?"

"Time is not known here, Kanoa. Come, the islanders have prepared your home."

What an answer.

The Mentor

THE RITUAL OF PREPARATION

We climbed to a ledge outside a cave thirty yards above the fire. I knelt and looked in, and when I looked back, Malu was gone. Nothing surprised me anymore.

I crawled into the domed cavern and saw a mat next to a fire and a life-sized stickman chipped into the wall on the other side of the flame. I walked to the symbol and traced its groove with my finger. "I guess we all do this."

That night I dreamed I was bobbing on my briefcase in the middle of a flat ocean when the water under me opened and I was swallowed by a toothless mouth. I clawed my way down an esophagus and landed on the wiggly pearl beach, and when I looked out, the ocean and waves were frozen. Suddenly the water cracked and the large man from my dream slowly rose out standing on the silver wing — the journal tucked under his arm. He started clapping. The claps were firecrackers. I covered my ears but it didn't help; then I woke up. The morning streamed into the cave, and I heard chopping coming from outside.

"What a night." I crawled onto the ledge and saw Malu hacking the log with a machete. Behind him were flowers and fruit laying on wide green leaves next to fish jammed on a spear stuck in the sand. He gestured and I climbed down.

"Aloha, Kanoa. How was your sleep?" he asked as he squatted and rolled some fruit, flowers, and a fish into a leaf then tied it with a vine.

"Well, I had this dream."

"Was it a good dream?" He kept rolling.

"I'm not sure. I don't know what it meant." I knelt and copied Malu.

"Leave one fish on the spear," he said.

Then we washed our hands in the saltwater and sat where we were the night before.

"Kanoa," Malu began, "the ritual of he'e nalu prepares your mind, body, and soul to ride the great wave beyond the cove. Do you remember how you felt before coming here?"

"How do you mean?"

"Was your life full?"

I thought it was a tricky question and wanted to challenge what the word *full* meant, but the answer was obvious. "No, I guess it wasn't, but I wanted to think it was. That's what we all do."

Chapter 11: The Ritual of Preparation

His eyes widened and he nodded.

"Kanoa, your life dreams come from a spirit speaking to you just as Kane spoke to the prince in the fable I told." He turned toward the cove and made motions with his hand. "See how the breeze blowing from the land kisses and holds the waves and makes them smooth?"

"Yes."

"Your grandfather taught that the voice of purpose and love blows within that *offshore breeze,* but that is not the one you are feeling or hearing. You and the students who come to Tronahu feel the wind from the ocean, the one that makes the waves rough and unrideable. This *onshore breeze* carries the voice and emotions of discontent that most people ignore.

"Instead, Kanoa," he gestured toward the shore, "they remain on the beach of the ordinary and never dare begin their journey to discover the magic in the freedom of he'e nalu."

He was right. My onshore breeze had been blowing a long time, but I blocked it with work and kidded myself that everything was all right. It wasn't.

"Kanoa, your grandfather met students here each morning. He taught that although the mind, body, and soul live within the same kingdom, the mind is the ruler."

Malu stood, then bent his knees, bowed his back, and held his hands out like claws.

"Your grandfather growled, '*It is the conscious mind that makes the choices of your life.* You can be a beast caged in yesterday's habits and instincts and run for shelter when a storm blows, or

Part Two: Trials and Principles

be a leader and paddle into the squall to seek the knowledge of its source.' Do you understand what he meant, Kanoa?" His claws were still up. "The animal lives in fear of change and counts the minutes to the same life, but a true king *lives* the moment to create a better future for those he serves."

I watched Malu the animal and remembered a chill as he stood and stretched.

"Come," he said.

We walked along the shoreline and stopped next to a clear pool rimmed with red-green coral. Malu squatted and motioned for me to join him.

"What do you see?" he asked.

I saw my reflection and thought it was odd he used the word *what* rather then *who*. I knew he was waiting for an answer, so I settled for, "Me."

"Kanoa, what you see are the eyes that were given the gift of 29,200 sunrises. What you see is the vehicle the gods have given you to discover and experience those moments."

He stood and faced the horizon.

"Your ancestors lived each day to ride those waves, and it was the lessons and trials of doing what they loved that molded and strengthened their beliefs and bodies.

"Your grandfather told the students, 'Look at what *you are* and know that *a frail body leads to a life and mind of chaos* and will never take you beyond the cove of monotony.'

"Here is where their training began and where it will begin for you tomorrow. Kanoa, see how the water near us is calm,

Chapter 11: The Ritual of Preparation

and farther out, waves break on the inside of the entrance? See the three rocks?" he asked.

"Yes."

"Each is twice the distance from the one before it."

I saw a rock shaped like an upside down boot sticking out of the water sixty yards from me and two smaller ones farther out. Swells broke on the third rock, and then fanned out, left and right.

"You will get to know those rocks very well. If you are going to take the surfboard beyond the cove, you must be stronger and smarter than the waves."

"How do I do that?"

"First, you must become a strong swimmer," he said. "Tomorrow you will swim to the first rock and back to the beach. Then when you feel ready, you will do the same to the second rock and then the third."

I thought for a second. "How will I know it's time to swim to the next rock? I mean, how many times do I have to swim to a rock and back every day to be ready for the next one?" I wanted specifics, a plan. Get it right.

"I cannot tell you that. Every person is different."

I winced.

"Kanoa, it is not about numbers or measuring. All I can tell you is what your grandfather taught us."

My grandfather, here we go. "What did he say?"

"'Your shadow will speak to you.'"

"Oh," I said. But that wasn't the answer I wanted, so I tried again. "So, you're telling me I'm going to have to swim to the third rock, through that white stuff, and I don't really know whether I'm ready or not? What happened to the idea of the surfboard? That's what I'm supposed to be using, right?"

"Being prepared means you must be ready for the unforeseen. If you lose your surfboard, only your swimming will save you."

"Save me?" I repeated, hoping Malu would laugh and say something like *not really*, but the begging-for-an answer face didn't change his concentration.

"There is another thing, Kanoa."

Here comes more.

"To ride the surfboard will require balance and strength that you cannot gain from swimming. Notice that the top of each rock is flat." He drew a picture in the air.

"Yeah, I see that."

"Each has notches, steps placed by the gods," he said. "To gain the balance required to ride the surfboard, each time you swim to the rock you will climb to the top and stand like this."

Malu held out his arms, spread his legs, and squatted sideways. "This is the heʻe position. Try it," he said.

Thirty seconds into the stance my thighs quivered and caught fire. I stood up. Malu was still in position.

"You are ready for the surfboard when you can swim to the third rock many times without effort and your legs no longer speak."

Malu stood, no pain. "We will talk after we honor Kane," he said. "Come, do as I do."

Chapter 11: The Ritual of Preparation

We placed the rolled leaves on the stickman symbol, raised our hands to Kane then knelt for several minutes and returned to the fire.

I watched Malu turn the last fish on the spear six inches from embers. Its skin bubbled and browned, and the smoke puffed then disappeared over the cove. He sliced the fish on the log then handed me half on a frond.

"Eat," he said

I picked, and once I was sure I wasn't going to gag on a bone, the meat was gone and it wasn't enough; but I didn't say anything. I leaned back on my elbows and closed my eyes; no car horns, just the ocean.

"Kanoa, do you remember evil Kanaloa in the fable I told?"

"Yes, of course."

"When the storm took your grandfather, it stole the people's soul, just like Kanaloa stole the Princess Kailani's soul. And just as Prince Kanoa lost his will, the people live in fear of another storm."

"So that's why the cove is empty," I said.

"True. No one has worshipped here since the hurricane."

I knew Malu was going somewhere with his process and I also knew that thinking medically and rationally about souls and fear wouldn't work here.

"Your grandfather taught that *your soul is the unconscious voice of your life's Spirit*. Unlike your body, it lives forever in the actions of those you teach, touch, and lead. He would tell the fable then say to the students, 'Without your soul, you wander

Part Two: Trials and Principles

the island of the ordinary, picking up empty shells of purpose and piling them on the *beach of same* in false satisfaction.'"

Ouch. I saw a pile of conch shells on my desk.

"Kanoa, your mind is prepared by being conscious of your choices, and your body by the ritual of the rocks, but your soul is different. You cannot call your soul on a whim; *it* chooses its time. You will feel its words when you are challenged to choose between evil and good and when your body says quit. Your soul will guide you through your trials on Tronahu, Kanoa, and help you answer the great question."

That was a lead-in and I knew he wanted me to ask, so I did, "What question?"

Malu grinned. "What would you be if you were not circling your island, plucking empty shells?"

I swallowed, and when enough time passed to justify the fact that I didn't have an answer, Malu nodded.

"Come, I know you are still hungry. We will go to the fishpond and I will teach you to throw the spear and net, then show you where to pick fruit. Tomorrow you swim."

The Ritual of Preparation

The Ritual of Preparation

THE ROCKS

We walked to the reflection pool the next morning.

"Remember what you are to do?" Malu asked.

"Swim to the first rock, climb up, do the he'e stance as long as I can, then swim back and keep repeating until I'm too tired. Right?"

"Good. You may begin," he said. "I will watch."

I waded in and when I reached the rock, I climbed to the top and lay on my stomach. The surface was dry, the size of an ironing board. I pulled myself to my knees and looked toward the beach. Malu extended his arms and crouched. I eased up sideways with my legs wide and squatted and flapped my arms like a seagull. Balance.

"One, two," I counted until my thighs screamed, then climbed down, swam to the beach, and started again. By the third try I was sucking air, my heart hammered, the thigh burn flamed at ten seconds, and my swim was floppy arms and backstrokes. When I reached shore I crawled five yards then rolled onto my back at Malu's feet.

"Not bad," he said

"I only made it three times," I said

"We all must begin our journey, Kanoa. Your grandfather taught that *those rocks are like the goals that lead to a life of meaning.* One must reach each to ride the great wave of purpose. People fail because they swim to the rock once and announce its defeat without taking time to learn the stamina, skills, and wisdom needed to swim beyond their earthly desires. Your grandfather promised that if you follow your ritual each day, you will experience a life and song you have been too busy to live or hear."

We returned to the fire, rolled the sacrifice leaves and placed them on the he'e symbol. Malu raised his hands and stared, so I did the same. Ten minutes passed.

"Can you see it?" he asked.

"See it?"

"See the wave?"

"What? Not really." I wasn't sure what he was talking about.

"Come, we will fish, then eat."

And so my ritual began. Each morning, I scratched a day notch into the cave wall and then swam, and then Malu and I placed the offering

"See the wave?" he would ask.

"I'm trying," I would say. I finally figured out what he was asking, but my thoughts scampered to questions and pictures.

Chapter 12: The Rocks

The swim to the first rock became effortless and the heʻe stance reached three minutes, so I decided to try for the second rock. It was like starting over, but I knew it would get easier with repetition, patience, and Malu's mentoring.

The day notches covered the cave wall, and one night I dreamed of the third rock and took it as a message from the gods. That morning I swam past the second rock, pushed into the white water, and by the time I reached the third rock, my chest was a balloon. I bobbed and hid behind the rock and let the froth seeth around me.

Once I caught my breath, I pulled myself to the first notch, strained to hold on until the next wave passed, then grabbed the next one. The top was a wet balance beam, so I scooted on my stomach as water hit my face. I held my breath and timed the waves, then jumped into the heʻe stance. The next wave was small but angry and slapped my chest and threw me backward. The water impact took my air, and an eddy twirled me under. I groped but the rock was gone, so I fought to the surface and choked in the foam and pawed like a wet dog. *I'll be okay*, I reminded myself. *Calm down and swim.*

The undercurrent pushed me out of the fizz to the center of the cove. I swam left and clung to the first rock and rested with my head back, gasping like a fish. When I reached the shallows, Malu was waiting.

"Where were you?" I stomped out of the water. "I almost drowned."

"You did well. You reached your goal."

Part Two: Trials and Principles

"You didn't tell me how powerful those waves are, Malu. Man, I really, really wasn't ready for that."

Malu squeezed my arms. I hung my head, embarrassed that I had lost control, then sat in the sand and hugged my knees.

"Sorry. What do I do now?" I asked.

"You build your surfboard."

I looked toward the tree trunk Malu had been carving. "That one?" I asked.

"No, Kanoa, that is mine."

I looked up; his eyes were twinkling.

"There is a secret in creating your own."

"Okay, then. Okay." I did one push-up, hopped to my feet, marched to the water, and swam out.

THE VISION

The next morning after I swam, Malu was waiting on the beach. He held a burlap bag in one hand and a belted machete in the other.

"In one hour, we will go into the high forest to find a koa tree to build your surfboard."

He handed me the knife.

"You will need this and your backpack."

We followed a path to the inner island and stopped where it divided into three. One curved toward a valley, the second into thick woods, and the third up toward the volcano.

"You will go from here. Follow the path into the forest."

"What do you mean?"

"This is your journey."

"You're leaving me here?" I looked around then back at Malu. "How do I know what tree to cut?"

"You will know," he said as he stuffed the burlap bag in my backpack.

"What's in the bag?"

"*Kumu*, a red fish."

"A fish?" I thought he was kidding. I was wrong.

"You must pay for the life of the tree, Kanoa. Remember, its spirit will be with you when you ride the great wave. When you find the tree, bury the fish at its roots, honor its gift and then chip it to the size of the one on the beach and bring it to me.

Until now I had accepted the oddity of this journey, but this was another level. Malu knew what I was thinking, but his quiet face reassured me.

"You must go," Malu said. He shooed me then vanished down the path.

I didn't know what to do, so I started walking with no idea what I was looking for; but as usual, that changed.

The path thinned into an animal trail in the high woods where the trees had thick trunks and sickle-shaped leaves with little yellow flowers. I stopped and spun around.

"Okay spirits, what now?" They answered.

It was faint — a fluorescent green in the woods to my right. I touched my belt and watched as the glow brightened, then saw the outline of the Stickman. The figure beckoned and faded, so I pulled out my machete and hacked into the overgrowth. There was no path, so I kept chopping. I felt every hack, every scratch.

Hours passed. I followed glimpses of the flickering to a clearing, sat against a log, pillowed my backpack, then scooched

Chapter 13: The Vision

onto my back and closed my eyes. Raindrops filtered through the canopy and ran down my face and into my mouth.

"Can you see it?"

I opened my eyes. The Stickman was sitting on the log three feet from me; it had no mouth or nose, just round blue eyes.

"Kanoa, the voice that called your ancestors is summoning you to begin the journey of he'e nalu, to seek and ride your perfect wave."

A dream. No, a delusion.

"Can you see it? It is the wave called life, the swell you and those whom you will mentor are destined to catch and experience beyond the touchable world. *The time has come to shed the old ideals and learn what you are.* It is time to walk the beach of hope and enter the cave of your soul to begin the ritual of rebirth.

"Can you hear it, Kanoa? Neither you nor those you will lead were meant to live on an island of fear and inaction. You were created to teach and share the vision of freedom that breaks on the reef beyond the confines of the meaningless cove of the ordinary. Listen. It is not one voice you hear, it is a harmony from the spirits of those who wait for their king."

I was cold, trembling.

"You must become the hero in the living fable that stirs the hearts of followers, the king that rode the impossible wave and cut the tongue of dragons to save the people. You must become the legend of stories told in the night to stir the imagination of children. You must become the truth-filled whisper in the offshore breeze that will lead others to their perfect wave."

Part Two: Trials and Principles

The Stickman faded. "See it, Kanoa."

Suddenly I saw myself paddling into a wall of water, I stand and drop on a gleaming surfboard. The wave becomes a green monster, howling and spitting, but I clench my teeth and laugh. It's mouth covers me; darkness, but it doesn't catch me this time. I blow into a white sun and soar into the clouds and I'm full and happy. It was all so clear.

I jerked awake in the he'e position with my palm pressed against a tree in the center of the clearing.

"I know you," I whispered. *We are one* flashed deep in my being.

I buried the kumu between the fingers of the roots and raised my machete, hesitated, then plunged the blade into the ground.

"Thank you, great spirit," I said. "Thank you for the gift of promise in the heart of this tree."

The Vision

14

THE SURFBOARD

The next afternoon, my tree lay next to Malu's half-shaped trunk. He had placed one of my grandfather's surfboards next to it, and after my swim, he handed me a lumpy leather bag.

"These were your grandfather's tools," he said.

I laid the knives and stones along my log.

"Each tool has a purpose, just like us. Use the blades to cut the rough shape and then smooth it with the pumice."

I stared at the gadgets, then ran my hand down my grandfather's board. The nose was up-curved and the tail tapered to a square. The fin was sharp on the rear edges. It all made sense.

"Kanoa, your grandfather taught the three parts of the board as if they were part of us: *the body, the fin, and the leash.*"

"The body of the board represents the *core of knowledge* one must have to adapt and survive the monsters and tsunamis in our journey. He would say to the students, 'Living yesterday's beliefs will yield the mundane and passionless rituals of an ordinary life.'

"Then he would have the students do as you have done, touch and stroke the board, and he would say, 'Too many are deaf to the meaning of the whisper in their onshore breeze. *They wake each day and paddle the same board of knowledge into their protected cove* and ride the easy waves then return to shore and scream *I have changed.*' Then he would lower his voice and say, 'They have not, they have not.'

"You see, Kanoa, your grandfather knew that most people never gain the insight and inspiration found in a journey beyond the harbor of their self-imposed limitations. They quit paddling, they stop learning, and they never discover the richness and freedom of a boundless existence."

I knew he was speaking to me, but there was something about his tone.

"What do you believe, Kanoa?"

A zinger. "About what, Malu?"

"About life, about work, about people?"

I struggled. "People are good," I said. "They want to live healthy, happy, meaningful lives." I stopped, caught in a thought, but it came out a question, and it wasn't to Malu. "Isn't that what I'm supposed be doing, helping them do that, live a good life? Is that what I believe? Why don't I know that? Am I doing that?" Rambling.

Chapter 14: The Surfboard

Malu watched until I stopped, then touched the fin. "Your grandfather called this the *fin of philosophy* because it gave direction to the board of knowledge. Remember, Kanoa, until the gods touched the genius of one man, your ancestors slid and fell when waves became mountains. After the fin was added, their philosophy about what they could do changed forever. They left the beliefs of their ancestors, experimented and learned, and became closer to what they loved."

I thought, *what they loved.*

"Your grandfather said to the students, 'You are like finless surfboards, lost souls slipping down the wave of life on worn and limiting beliefs.' His teachings gave them their fin and sent them in the direction of their perfect wave."

"But remember, " he said, "the fin of philosophy only takes you in the direction of your beliefs. The monster, Kanaloa, saw the world through red eyes of greed and mimicked change to impose its will over others. It believed it should own the ocean and control every life and every kumu. It lived on impulse, Kanoa, and sought to shackle the souls of those who threatened to speak their dreams. Unlike your fin of philosophy, the creature held a thirst for a power that could never be quenched. In the fable you

Part Two: Trials and Principles

can see what Kanaloa believes by the way the creature treated the islanders and the princess."

His lips thinned and he shook his head.

"Stay here."

He strode to a sack on the ground and pulled out a looped rope and threw it to me. It was frayed and I knew what it was, but I wasn't sure it would work.

"Your grandfather's first leash," he said. "He made many, each one better, until he got rubber from the mainland."

He motioned and I tossed him the rope.

"He called this the *leash of discipline* because it binds you to your board of knowledge and fin of philosophy."

What a metaphor, I thought.

"He would waggle it in front of the students and say, 'You may gain the knowledge of a king and claim the purpose of great philosophers, *but little is done if you do not have the discipline to go to the water each day.*' Then he twirled it like this."

Malu spun it over his head like a lasso.

"Do you hear that?" Whoop, whoop, whoop. "That is the sound of the heart of your perfect wave, Kanoa. That is where great leaders and kings discover what they are."

He stopped and the lasso dangled next to his thigh.

"But Kanoa, getting to your perfect wave is not easy. Your grandfather taught that if you yield to the ease of *later* and *tomorrow* and *maybe,* you would never see the potential in each dancing sunray. He stood here and asked the students, 'How many times have you closed the windows to quiet the whisper

Chapter 14: The Surfboard

in your onshore breeze and waited for the hot breath of Kanaloa to wake you with an invitation to a life of low expectation?'"

Man, I thought, when did that happen? When did I go from trying to accepting, when did I go from doing what was right to giving in?

Malu pulled the leash taught across his chest then turned toward the rocks in the cove. "He taught the students that each morning they must walk into the mist of first light and paddle to the first rock, then again, back and forth, Kanoa; and he would say, 'When your body cries out, yank your leash of discipline and stroke harder and faster because **what you are** *lies in the extreme,* that is where the moral character and confidence of a king is molded.'"

He handed me the leash.

"You must build your own surfboard, Kanoa. Look at your hands."

I looked down and spread my fingers then made a fist.

"Within those hands lie the knowledge, philosophy, discipline, and wisdom of all the kings and surfers who dared to paddle into the storm of their time. They are here. They are here, Kanoa, building your board with you so you will not face the trials of he'e nalu alone."

An onshore breeze gusted, I picked up the knife. "I'm ready."

Each day after my swim, I stood on the stickman etching and spoke to Kane and saw the vision from the forest. Each afternoon, Malu watched me trim and smooth the plank and pressed his hand on mine to teach the correct pressure and motion. We painted the finished shape with white sap we drained from trees and wrapped the board in elephant leaves, then buried it to cure in the sand near a freshwater stream. After we were done we placed our sticky hands on each other's shoulders like kid buddies.

"It will be ready in three weeks," Malu said. "You should be proud, Kanoa. It will be a good board."

"Yes, it will be a good board."

The Surfboard

THE WHITEWATER

I stood in the reflection pool and steadied the koa board with one hand, and listened to Malu.

"This ritual is the same except for one thing," he said. "Instead of standing on the rock, you will balance on the board. You will still swim each day, and then you will paddle to the first two rocks until you are ready for the third. Each uses different muscles. Do you understand?"

"Yes."

"Then go."

I shoved the board and jumped. My ribs bounced against the deck, and I arched my back and reached with my right arm. The only noise was the splash of my hands.

"This is easy," I said when I reached the first rock. Malu watched.

I straddled the board, then wiggled to one knee and grasped the rails. When the board stopped rocking I stood halfway, but it tilted and lurched then rolled me off the tail. Not so easy. On the fifth attempt, I turned sideways on my knees, then eased to a low squatting position with my feet so wide my groin groaned. I wobbled, then eased up and down in the stickman stance three times before slipping.

"I know this game." Keep trying and adjusting, and sooner or later I'll get it. I followed the ritual every day: swimming, paddling, offering, fishing, and each night I rubbed some kukuinut oil into the board to prevent waterlogging.

One morning I announced to Malu, "Today I'm going through the breakers and surf my first wave."

"Then you must try," he said.

I paddled past the second rock and over the heave of dying swells, then kept stroking. The early whitewater was an easy foam, but farther out it plowed into my chest and knocked me backwards. I clenched my teeth, shoved my arms deep, and pushed past the shoulder ache. Forty-five minutes later I was a rag doll, clinging to my life raft board in the calm next to first rock.

"You know, your grandfather had a great sense of humor," Malu said as he paddled next to me in a canoe.

"He would have thought this was funny?" I asked. "You knew this would happen."

"The future cannot be predicted, only discovered."

"Is that another one of my grandfather's sayings?"

Chapter 15: The Whitewater

"Maybe." He hesitated while I bobbed. "When you are ready, we will honor the gods, then talk."

I rested my cheek on the board and paddled in twenty minutes later.

After we fed Kane, Malu surprised me with tuna and a gourd of coconut water. Instead of returning to the beach, we dangled our legs in the water next to the he'e symbol and ate in silence.

"All the work I've done, and I can't even get past the breakers," I said. I sounded like a baby but didn't care.

"Your grandfather would have asked why you kept paddling into the whitewater when you were not progressing."

"That's what you taught me." My voice hitched.

"I taught you to paddle the surfboard. You are a doctor, right?"

Where's he going now?

"Do you treat all your patients the same?"

"No. I get it. I should have tried something different, but it's a little hard to think of that when you're getting slammed in the face."

"Kanoa, look around. Do you know where you are?"

I rolled my shoulders and stared at the third rock.

"Your grandfather taught that too many waste time on the beach hugging their board of knowledge and adjusting their fin of philosophy. They strap and unstrap their leash of discipline while they watch others ride the waves. They paddle out and are beaten by the power of the whitewater and of those who wish to push them back to their shore of same and to control their destiny."

"Like me this morning." I made that comment to myself.

"Yes and no," he said. "Those who repeatedly try and fail are using force over strategy. They ride back to the beach on their belly, convinced they are not worthy, then grow old collecting empty shells, wondering what they lacked that the others knew."

I looked at Malu. "So what did my grandfather teach? What's the secret?"

Malu twisted. "He taught that they lacked nothing except the resolve and creative innovation the others had used to fool Kanaloa's whitewater."

I thought that answer was too simple but had learned that the limitations to understanding the meaning of Malu's lessons was my problem, and figuring them out was the grand scheme of my journey.

"Kanoa, you have learned that no matter the planning and preparation in the small waves of the cove, no one is prepared for Kanaloa's cunning. Each day, swell, and current is different. Your grandfather's favorite saying was that *'a king and leader's greatest transformation and self-discovery occurs in their fight for survival.'* The students learned, as you will learn, that only a hero's intention will carry you past the threshold of the ordinary.

"I promise, Kanoa, that once you see the world beyond the whitewater, the imagination hiding in your shadow will speak,

Chapter 15: The Whitewater

and you will never return to the *island of same* nor be what you once were."

I thought about the word survival and the fact that I'd paddled nowhere for the past few years, maybe longer. We sat in the heat until the tide washed around us, then stood and watched Kane's bouquets float into the cove.

"Come, Kanoa, it is time to rest and think about this morning's lesson," Malu said. "This afternoon you will begin again, only this time you will seek to understand the force of the whitewater and where it is striking you. The answer is in here." Malu pressed his temple.

I slept in the shade of a bush growing through a crack in the wall behind the fishpond. The wind was calm and the sun was dying when I paddled into the slush of the third rock. The force shoved me back, so I tried again. Only this time, just before the water hit me, I pushed up, and the froth rolled under my chest.

"Easier," I said. Timing is critical. The push-up was effective until I reached the reef where the break cracked, but I had a plan. As the next wave broke I flipped the board and hung on underwater as the whitewater washed over the bottom. Flip then paddle, flip then paddle. It worked. Do it again. One more stroke and I cruised over an unbroken face and slapped into a trough. I pumped my fists, then scanned for Malu's canoe. I was alone.

I pushed the heels of my palms into my thighs and inhaled. The empty beach reminded me of Malu's lesson: "You must be prepared to face the storms alone." I paddled out farther and waited, my neck thumped. A swell rolled toward me. Here goes — I slow stroked toward the beach then dug faster. The board surged, and I pushed and stood in one motion. I was the Stickman! I rode straight and fell into the deep water between the second and third rock.

He'e nalu, my first wave, like my first baby step, my first word. A miracle! *Aoooo.* No one heard me. I stood again and again until the light was dim and a star hung above the cliff. The last wave . . . watch this. I paddled at a right angle then stood and leaned and slid across the smooth face into the center of the cove. The gods smiled as my laugh echoed in the cove.

"*Ha! I am a surfer.*"

The
Whitewater

16

MEETING EVIL

Weeks passed and I practiced left and right, experiencing the difference between the speed and power of the larger and smaller waves. I learned the effects of the wind and the risk of bare reefs at low tide. Catching the swells became easy, every ride a thrill and experiment. One afternoon when the surf was medium, I saw a swirl near the third rock, probably a dolphin. I swung the board in an arc and checked the water beneath me, then farther out. Nothing. It's nothing.

A wave rolled in and I took three strokes. Suddenly something hit the bottom of the board and bucked me into the water then brushed my face and chest. I scrambled. My skin was burning. Red welts streaked down my left arm.

"Oh, man." I bolted for shore, and by the time I stepped on the beach, my skin was blistered and my eyes were swollen slits. My throat tightened and I tossed my board and ran.

Part Two: Trials and Principles

Where is Malu? I crawled into the cave and poured a skein of water over my head. My chest was in a vice. I needed oxygen; stay calm, just stay calm. Where is Malu? My legs shook when I tried to stand.

I wriggled to the mat and lay on my back and took shallow breaths. I gurgled, "help." Then the cave spun and I held onto the floor as the dome blurred. I'm dying. I saw a form with red eyes above me.

"Go."

All went dark; I was dead.

Something touched my face. I opened my eyes and saw a woman holding a white feather kneeling next to me. Her hair was silver and long, but her blue eyes were young. She smiled and wiped my forehead.

"Wake up, Kanoa," she said.

I couldn't move. Was I paralyzed? I closed my eyes and felt fingertips stroke my cheeks.

"Wake up, Kanoa."

I rolled my eyeballs under my lids then wiggled my fingers. I took a breath and held it for a few seconds, then wheezed it out. Once I was sure I could breath I tried to see, but the sunlight cutting across the cave blinded me, so I put my hands over my face and peeked between my fingers until everything adjusted.

"What a dream." I huffed twice then raised my head. A blanket covered me, so I pulled it off and struggled to my elbows. I was caked in clay that cracked as I moved, and surrounded by ten black stones the size of marbles. An urn was

Chapter 16: Meeting Evil

next to the fire. I sat up and peeled the clay then made it to my hands and knees.

"You have met Kanaloa." I saw Malu leaning against the stickman etching, holding my grandfather's journal.

"Malu." My voice was air. "What happened? Something stung me, I couldn't breathe."

"You have met Kanaloa."

"What? You said it was a myth. Are you telling me there's a squid thing in the cove?"

"It does not want you here." He picked up the stones and dropped them in a drawstring bag then shook the blanket. The stickman was woven into its center.

"Who put the paste on me?" I hung my head. "Come on, Malu, tell me what's going on."

"Not everyone is ethical," he said. "Your grandfather warned of creatures that are driven by the darkness of power and numbers of self-gain. They lurk beneath the waves or appear harmless until they sting. *You must decide whose world you join,* and that decision can never be hidden with blab. It will define what you are and whether or not you are respected by those who seek the same waves and opportunities as you."

A wave of nausea hit me and the room spun, so I jackknifed down and put my hand out. Stop. I heard a shuffle then Malu's fingers dug into the back of my neck. Silence. A voice. It wasn't Malu's.

"To rescue the spirit of that which you love, you must prove yourself worthy by learning the principles of he'e nalu and freeing those who wait for their king. You have announced your intentions by paddling out, Kanoa, and in doing so you have moved beyond the threshold of the ordinary where Kanaloa waits.

"You must understand that those who are watching feel the same emptiness and unanswered longing that once haunted your days. They see you with your hands raised to me and wonder if what *you* believe is what beats in *their* hearts. They wonder if you are their awaited leader or the false god that steals their hopes, then their princess.

"I will provide what you need to slay the monster hiding in your shadow, the amulets of power, the feather of flight, and the dagger of intention. It is time to paddle into your destiny, Kanoa. Now go."

When I raised my head, the spinning was gone and Malu had placed the journal and bag of stones on the folded stickman blanket next to the fire. He walked into the cone of light shooting through the entrance and knelt to leave.

"You will know when to open your grandfather's journal. It is a beautiful day. Kane is hungry. Go surf."

I should have said *are you kidding* or *no way*, but that would show weakness. I clenched my fists until the anger passed then guzzled water, rubbed my legs and stretched. Then I picked up the lava rock and walked to the wall: the day marks were scratched out. Huh.

After the offering, I watched the waves hit the third rock, and I knew something in me had changed. That night Kanaloa taunted me in a nightmare; the creature screamed and slammed

Chapter 16: Meeting Evil

its tail outside the cove entrance. I awoke exhausted and lay on my side, staring at the blanket, book, and bag of stones Malu had left.

"This is crazy." I sat on the blanket and placed the stones around me. Each was different and each engraved with the stickman symbol. I waited. A blue spark jumped from one, so I held it in the light. A kaleidoscope.

"Wow."

I dropped the other stones back in the bag, grabbed my surfboard and walked to Kane's rock.

"You will never beat me." I threw the stone and watched the splash. Just when I thought nothing would happen, the water boiled, and a twenty-foot geyser shot into the air, as rainbow ripples spread until the cove was a motion of color.

"Warrior," I said. I threw my fist into the air. "Warrior." Then I tossed my board into the fantasy and paddled out.

Meeting Evil

Meeting Evil

FOCUS AND CRISIS

I resumed the ritual and surfed in the morning and evening. My days were automatic, and I replayed the waves that threw me and learned and improved. I wasn't lonely. Thoughts of wading into the fray of medicine were suppressed by fast, deep strokes and adrenaline. I told myself that I was getting better but wasn't ready for the big waves, not yet. I never saw Malu, but I knew he was watching. I assumed he would show up when it was time to try something different. I was wrong.

One afternoon I cleaned fish then paddled out for a last session. I turned when a wisp of air grazed my neck and saw a thunderhead on the horizon. Something's up. Suddenly the sun was gone and a blast of wind rocked me. I saw a rift in the clouds moving toward the island. Wrong again; it was the crest of a mountain of water. I knew there wasn't time to make it to shore, so I whipped my board into the squall. Sideways raindrops blinded me and stung like arrows. I thought I could hide behind the rocks near the mouth of the cove, but the gale held me in place, so I kept stroking and hoping I could get over the swell before it broke. Too late.

The wave breached the barrier into the cove. I climbed straight up; I was in trouble. Just as I reached the crest, the peak feathered, and a water claw grabbed my board and threw me. I death-gripped my arms and legs around the board in a backward free fall; and just before I hit the water, the lip caught up and punched me into the reef, stood on my chest, and raked me across the coral.

I was disoriented. My lungs were exploding. I heard a voice: *the leash*. I grabbed and yanked then kicked and blasted into oxygen. "Ahhh." I sucked in one breath just as another wave bashed me into the bottom, so I relaxed to save oxygen and let the current carry me to the deep water.

I popped up in the middle of the cove and saw my leash attached to the back third of my busted board, so I tucked the chunk under my chest and kicked into the shallows then sat on the beach.

My back was burning, and gashes on my feet were plugged with sand. The sun came out and the cove was quiet as if nothing had happened. I limped down the shoreline and found the rest of my board, and I threw the pieces in the sand below the cave and went inside. I slathered the cuts with the paste from the urn and lay facedown on the mat.

Chapter 17: Focus and Crisis

I glanced across the floor and saw a white feather protruding from of my grandfather's journal and had a flash of the bird and the old lady.

"I guess it's time."

I stretched for the book and thumbed through the pages. They were blank except for the stickman symbol on the corner of the one marked by the feather. Here it comes, I thought. The quill flew into the air, spun over the journal and wrote like a pen.

> For the first time since you first paddled out you are no longer in control of your destiny, no longer making the decisions, and no longer chasing your bliss. You have become too comfortable wrapped in thoughts of the waves of yesterday, blind to the horizon of possibilities and the dangers of today and tomorrow. You are no longer preparing, planning, and improving for the future challenge of a king's leadership and service. You have become like the others, conforming to their culture instead of challenging your own. You have lost the focus and ambition necessary to ride your dream wave.
>
> Grandson, the ocean of life is not simple; the tides, currents, and drift will pull

you from the reef of your true potential, and the effort of one's attention tires quickly. The difference between a king and those on the beach is the ability to tune out the chatter in the onshore wind. You must first concentrate on what you are becoming and the value-based decisions that will yield the authentic actions of the people's hero. Then, you must reach out and feel the pulse of those islanders and families who have been waiting for your voice, those you have forgotten in the laxity of self-indulgence.

Remember, you are not just the hope of the island of Tronahu, you are a global messenger, and after you have checked your intuition and intentions and gone back to the villages, you must see that the energy in the stickman symbol of he'e nalu is released to the universe. Grandson, you must teach the students that even after they have ridden the great wave beyond the cove, they must continue to focus on what they are. There is more than one perfect wave.

Chapter 17: Focus and Crisis

The feather faded as the journal closed. I put the book on the floor and lay with the rolled stickman blanket under my chin. Everything hit me; the pain, the reality, the embarrassment. My lips quivered.

"Just when I was feeling safe."

"You are safe."

I jerked. Someone touched my back.

"Lay still. Those are pretty good cuts."

I tried to roll over.

"Stay where you are, John Kanoa."

"Kala? What are you doing here?" It didn't make sense.

"Saving you. Now don't move." She spread the paste on my back; her hands were soft and careful.

"No, I mean how did you know I was here?"

"Everybody knows you're here."

"You're kidding."

"I brought you a treat," she said.

I sat up and she poured coffee from a thermos.

"Are you real?"

She ignored my question and handed me the cup.

"I remembered you drank it black, that should be real enough for you."

"Thank you."

"You mean mahalo."

"Mahalo." The coffee was nectar. "This is the best coffee I've ever had."

"It's our own coffee. The beans are grown on the side of the volcano, and we sell them all over the world, *Heavenly Tronahu Coffee.*"

"Was that my grandfather's idea?"

"Probably," she said. "Now, lie down." She covered me with the blanket and placed a flower under my palm. "I have to go."

"Is the flower magic?"

"Only if you think it is." I heard her steps. "You'll be all right. The gods are on your side. Sleep, then take time to heal and think." Then she was gone.

Focus and Crisis

Focus and Crisis

THE VOLCANO

When I woke up, the wounds and pain were gone.

"She's right, I need to go somewhere to figure this out."

I strapped on my machete and put the blanket, some bread, and a skein of water into my backpack. I didn't have a plan, so I followed Malu's path and stopped where it split into three. Which one? Does it matter? I closed my eyes and listened and remembered what Malu had said about my shadow. I chose the path toward the volcano. I don't know why.

I climbed, and late in the day the trail ended at the lip of what looked like an endless black parking lot. As I walked higher the sulfur burned my throat, so I rested against a boulder and drank water. I looked at my island; green fading into turquoise.

Part Two: Trials and Principles

"Hey Ken, can you see this?" I said. "Wish you were here, man, I could use your help right now." I turned; something, something, something on that volcano. "I hear you. I'm coming."

I hopped over fissures until sunset then spread the stickman blanket on the ground next to the only tree I could find. A fog dropped; it was the darkest night I had ever seen.

I thought about my two worlds; this surfing fantasyland and my overloaded schedule back home. "There's got to be more to life than that." I grimaced and fell asleep.

A boom woke me and an orange flash lit the fog. "Uh-oh. What now?" A brighter flash then the ground shuddered. "This better not be the volcano."

As I stood I saw the Stickman disappear into an arch in the mist twenty yards away. "Here we go again." I grabbed my stuff and followed the glow to a rim overlooking a crater of spitting lava surrounded by waterfalls that hissed into the mass.

"Welcome, Kanoa." A woman's voice.

"Who's there?"

"I am here."

I turned and saw the silver-haired woman in my dream.

"Do I know you?"

"Of course you do, Kanoa, I rocked you in the spirit of the sunrise." She touched my chin.

"Tutu." The name slipped from nowhere.

"Yes, I am your grandmother."

"Are you the one that's calling me?"

Chapter 18: The Volcano

"There are many voices calling, my child, including your own."

I struggled to find a word but knew one thing: I loved this woman and wanted to hug her, but I didn't.

"Come." She grasped my hand and we sat on a rock bench.

"This is a sacred place," she said. "The kings came here to speak with the gods. Your grandfather was gone for weeks, and when he returned he transformed the island."

"Then I guess that's why I'm here," I said. "I've lived another life, and here I am sitting on the edge of a volcano trying to decide what to do. It would be easy to sell the island so I can get back to what I know, but now all I want to do is surf and stay away from the whole mess. Then there's Malu and this crazy idea that I'm supposed to ride a giant wave to prove myself."

"Kanoa, my husband taught that the answers you seek already live within you." She squeezed my hand. "*The choices you make must be driven by your dream and what is right for the people you will touch and lead.* Whether or not you go back, leave the island to others, or ride the great wave, will be the choice only you can make. Your decision will come from your heart or will be shaped by forces outside yourself, some good and some evil."

"I've discovered evil."

"Kanoa, those guiding you know there is a mysterious longing that drives every hero surfer beyond the threshold of safety and survival. Such a yearning can never be held in your palm. Look at me."

Part Two: Trials and Principles

I saw the eyes that rocked me and watched her lips form the words.

"Broken boards never stopped your grandfather. He taught that a damaged board symbolized the need to move within and ask your shadow why you allowed Kanaloa to control your journey. He gave the students three choices.

"The first was to drag the pieces to their hut and let the voices of anxiety and helplessness melt the dream of their perfect wave: *That is called quitting.*

"The second was to repair their board and leave it weak, then move to a beach where the waves are less powerful, there is no risk, and where their perfect wave will never break. *That is called mediocrity.*

"And the third is to re-enter the forest, build a vehicle better suited to ride the great waves of purpose, then revisit the ritual of the rocks to prepare for the swell that will blot the horizon. *That is called perseverance.*"

I rested my head on her shoulder.

"Your grandfather was a great king because he did not decide for those who sought his wisdom," she said. "He gathered them on the beach and helped them paint their own picture of the miracles beyond the cove. Kanoa, you will see the spark of freedom in the students' eyes when you ask them to paddle out beside you, not behind you. You must go on, it is what you are called to do. Say, I will never quit."

"I will never quit."

"I will paddle out anyway."

Chapter 18: The Volcano

"I will paddle out anyway."

"Close your eyes," she said. "Shhh, listen to your shadow, it is time to rest." She hummed a melody I knew.

When I woke up I was laying on the bench, and the crater was black and silent and lit by a crown of twinkles. A kumu lay next to me. I meditated until dawn lit the rim, placed the fish in my backpack, then climbed down and chopped into the forest.

The Volcano

The Volcano

THE PERFECT WAVE

I faced the cove holding my new board; it was light, fast, and turned like a fish. The previous weeks I swam beyond the third rock, dove to the reef until I could hold my breath for minutes, and changed to a wider, lower stance.

"This is the day."

An offshore breeze tickled my back as I tied the satchel of nine stones to a rope around my waist. Malu dropped his arm around my shoulders.

"Kane and the spirits of the sun and the moon are with you," he said. "Remember what you are and what you have learned."

I touched his hand. Once past the third rock, I caught an aqua ribbon of outgoing current that carried me beyond the cove and through the shallows. In the distance I saw waves explode into forty-foot rainbows as they met the reef.

Part Two: Trials and Principles

"So this is what you look like." I made mental notes; the waves always break in one spot, the big ones break farther out, every wave tubes and dies once it hits the dark water on either side of the reef. The rights are better than the lefts.

Once I reached the deep water I paddled at an angle until I was sitting one hundred yards behind the break. I had two hours before the tide filled the reef, so I watched the hat-shaped shadow of the volcano creep from the cliffs to the foothills. An hour passed.

I saw a splash in the water thirty yards away and watched, but whatever it was disappeared. I paddled out farther, but when I stopped I saw bubbles around my board.

"No." I pulled my legs up, but it was too late. I was in the air, upside down. I landed on my back and struggled onto the board. I was too close to the breakers, they thundered and the steeper swells pulled me toward the drop-off. I spun with my arms and scrambled, but the bubbles returned and tossed me again. I knew I'd die if I went over. There was no plan, just reaction, survival. I jammed my arms deep and set my chin. When I was almost to safety a shape passed under my board.

"Come on!" I screamed and sat up. "Come on." The water swirled and there I was, face to face with lava-red eyes over a black beak surrounded by suction cup tentacles. It rolled and dove. I fumbled for the stones, but the bag was gone. Suddenly the water was black ink, and something grabbed my ankles and jerked me into an underwater tornado. I fought, but it pulled me deeper. It was dark and cold. I clamped my lips to save my

Chapter 19: The Perfect Wave

last breath then saw my adopted parents waving, then blue eyes; and just before the bubble exploded from my cheeks, something gripped my wrist and I heard Tutu's voice: *"Become the wave you are seeking, King Kanoa."*

Suddenly, nine streams of fire dropped around me, and I was walled in a spinning funnel of yellows and reds and blues. My lungs filled, and I pulled my board to my chest and splashed into an orange world where the sun and a full moon touched opposite horizons. I sagged forward and took deep breaths. I was alive.

"Kanoa, it is time to live your dream and learn your final lesson."

I looked up and saw a boy sitting on a flat wooden board.

"You saved me," I said.

"You saved yourself," he said. "What you have learned are the principles that guide the lives of those who seek *for* and not *from* others. We are not placed on this earth to own it or dominate what does not need to be confined. On your surfer's journey to ride that perfect wave of bliss, you have discovered that the emotional fluctuation of yearning and seeking and conquering can never be quenched with a mindset of *me*. The waves we seek are alive. They are power and energy and life, shaped into a visible form, just like you."

He gestured toward the open ocean.

"Unseen forces continuously transform the shape, direction, and power of all waves, but the purity of their spirit never changes. The wave understands it exists as a living piece of the ocean and the universe. Although one may feel the exhilaration of each ride, that elation, like life on earth, is short-lived, and the craving for more will never be satisfied. You have learned that the dream wave you were seeking has always existed in the potential hidden in your shadow and that the principles of heʻe nalu will endure as your guide through eternity.

"Kanoa, all great kings and leaders know the only truth that exists lies between the waves you hear, see, and feel, and the deep peace you discover in sharing a common journey with those whose purpose lies beyond the constriction of time and personal want."

He raised his outstretched arms toward the horizon, and a ghostly surfer appeared, then another, and another, until I was surrounded by hundreds of floating images. A beam shot from his hands and connected me to all the surfers; I was invincible, fearless, and unstoppable.

"Today, Kanoa, you will become the spirit of the wave. We surf."

I turned to a prism-tinged mass rolling toward me and paddled next to the boy while the spirits cheered. The swell lifted me and surged, and as it struck the shallows, I jumped to the heʻe stance and flew over the cliff toward the reef. The board skittered, and I pumped into the inverted waterfall as a roar announced the whitewater chasing me. I shifted forward and climbed high as the lip grazed my back, then I crouched in a tube of humming green phosphorus. "Ahhh," I screamed, and at the last second I rode the wind up and over as the section collapsed in a booming sigh. *I did it.*

The Perfect Wave

The Perfect Wave

PART THREE
Paddle In

**"You Are Not the Dr. John Foster
I Met in Los Angeles"**

THE MEETING

The Kuanset Corporation boardroom was decorated with potted palms and hula dancer posters. I sat next to Ben Graham at the end of a long table with businessmen and women dressed in Hawaiian shirts. Cecil Stone stood at the opposite end and pointed at a satellite picture of Tronahu.

"We've done our homework, Dr. Foster," he said. "Tronahu's economy is struggling, times have changed, and tourists want to see the old Hawaii. That's our goal. The dead volcano is a big draw not only for tourism, but also for archeologists who have been blocked from the island. We'll create jobs for the islanders, real jobs, and they'll be able to take their skills anywhere in the world. We'll build new schools and an international college right here." Cecil pointed to the area halfway up the volcano I had hiked with the kumu.

Part Three: Paddle In

"We know you're particularly concerned about the cove, and our goal is to keep it as untouched as possible. It's for snorkeling and swimming, fishing, and surfing, of course. We know your grandfather's resort had individual huts, and, although that's not financially feasible, the condominiums can be hidden in the trees away from the cove." He stopped and waited, so I nodded and he continued.

Stone tapped the pineapple fields. "This land is prime for an airport," he said. "Not too big, but large enough for moderate-sized airliners, especially the island hoppers. The runway will be far enough from the resort to limit the noise, and we'll fix the roads to handle the traffic. We want to leave the agriculture in place so that the people driving or taxiing will feel they've traveled back in time." He paused.

"The folks here are our implementation and management team," he said. "They've renovated historical sites all over the world, and they're especially excited about this project."

Each head smiled, so I smiled back.

"Doctor Foster, we know you've got a lot to think about. I put copies of our prospectus and a contract along with my personal phone number in your folder. Call me anytime for any reason."

It was my turn. "You're right, I've been gone a long time, and I need to get back to see what's left of my practice. Thank you, Mr. Stone, and thank you all for the presentation." They clapped and I walked outside with Ben and we stood next to a Kuanset limo.

"I'm not even going to ask." Ben said.

Chapter 20: The Meeting

"About what?" I waved for a taxi.

"About whatever happened on that island. You're not the Dr. John Foster I met in Los Angeles."

"You're right, that person no longer exists." I slid into the cab and winked. "I'll get back with you in a month or so."

The Meeting

HOME

I took a midnight flight home. My bed was too soft, so I slept under a sheet on a rug next to my bed. The next morning, Leah hugged me as I stepped off the elevator.

"You've got to let go sometime," I said.

She stepped back. "You're not going to stay, are you?"

"Give me a break, I just got back."

"No, hmmm . . . It's not the hair; it's your eyes. You've seen something."

"I've seen a lot and I've learned a lot," I said, "but I'm back."

"Okay then, let me know when you want to talk." We walked to my office. "It's clean, there's some mail, but that's about all. You start seeing patients in three days. They missed their Dr. Foster." She covered her mouth. "Oh, and there's a rumor that the new CEO, Mr. Akin, wants a word with you."

Part Three: Paddle In

"Thanks, Leah." She left and I walked to the window and looked at the city silhouette, then picked up a cellophane-wrapped basket of fruit from my desk. *Welcome Back* — the card was unsigned. One week passed.

It was two hours past my last patient when the phone rang.

"You have a visitor, Doctor Foster," Leah said.

"Right now?" I asked. "I've got a board meeting in twenty minutes." She didn't answer.

There was a tap and I couldn't get my feet under me before Kala walked in.

"Kala, what are you doing here?"

"Funny, you've asked me that before." She tilted her head. "I'm doing what I'm always doing, John Kanoa, saving your life." She tossed me a package. "Malu said you forgot this."

"I mean, what are you doing in the States?"

"I told you I have a business degree, Doctor, so I'm doing business. Let's just say I'm protecting the interests of my people."

"No, if you're asking, I haven't signed any contracts. I don't meet with Kuanset for a couple weeks." I was stalling.

Okay." She reached for the doorknob. "Malu said to tell you not to open the package right now. He said you'd know when. And hey, I know you're in a hurry, but don't forget what you are."

Click. I sat there, just sat there. At home that night I wrestled with dreams I don't remember, and the next morning at work I couldn't focus. *Ring . . .*

Chapter 21: Home

"Dr. Foster, this is Matt Akin. Welcome back."

"Thanks, Mr. Akin."

"Call me Matt, Doctor. Hey, I wonder if we can meet around two p.m. today. I already had Leah clear your schedule, hope that was all right."

"Sure Matt, that's fine. I'll see you then." My temples pounded.

At exactly two p.m. I knocked on Akin's door. No one answered, so I opened it. The CEO looked up from three computer screens, blinked, and then glanced at his watch.

"I'm John Foster. Are you Matt Akin?" I asked.

"Wow, it's two o'clock already?" He checked his watch again, then extended his hand. "Please have a seat, Dr. Foster. Sorry the room is so dark, I have trouble seeing the screens."

I sat in front of his desk.

"You've been on quite a vacation, I hear. To the Islands?"

"Well, not really a vacation."

"Yeah, yeah, my wife and I went to Honolulu for our honeymoon fifteen years ago."

"Did you surf?"

"No, we're not water people. You know, sharks and poisonous things like that." He turned to his computer and spoke without looking at me. "Well anyway, Doctor, we're glad you're back, but there are a couple things we need to talk about."

"What things?"

"Just some concerns the board members had." He clicked his mouse a few times. "Ah, there it is. I'll show you." He spun the screen.

Part Three: Paddle In

"Doctor, when I took over, I reviewed the productivity of all the doctors. That's my job," he said. "What I — we — noticed was that over the past twelve months the number of patients you have been seeing has dropped, and, of course, that affects our income; and, as you know, that's how we survive and grow. Can you help me understand what's going on?"

"Too much junk," I said and waited until he looked at me. "Just too much junk to do rather than take care of patients."

"You're talking about the new regulations and reporting?"

"That's part of it, yes." He knew this.

"No one likes it, but it's what we're forced to do," he said. "You and I know the numbers don't lie, right?"

I was smothering in yak.

"Doctor Foster, all we're asking is that you look at your schedule and just add one or two patients per day, that's all. And please, no more vacations for a while, at least until your productivity improves."

"What do you see?"

"I beg your pardon?"

"What do you see?" I asked. "What's your dream for this company? Better yet, what's your personal dream? What do you want to do with your life?"

"Well, well." He drummed the desk, stuck his bottom lip out and made a squirrel face. "Doctor, that's such an odd question I'm not sure how to respond. I — we've — got to work on that, I guess." The meeting was over.

Chapter 21: Home

That night I dreamed the entrance to the cave was blocked by an iron gate. I pounded until it creaked open and crawled in. The cavern was murky except for a spotlight on a desk under the stickman etching; my surfboard was in three pieces on the floor.

"I see you made it back from vacation," Matt Akin said as he spun in a chair behind the desk. His face was a computer screen with bloodshot eyes. Cecil Stone stood next to him wearing a tuxedo and a yellow-crested helmet.

"You're late." Stone said. "We've been waiting for your answer. Freedom." He grunted as he raked a claw across the stickman. Blisters popped out across my chest and a tentacle grabbed my throat. I choked. My legs gave out. I was on my knees. Stone's eyes rolled into flaming coals, and his mouth became a beak. "You're too weak to be king. Go back in your shell; Tronahu is mine." He cackled and flipped the journal into the fire.

Then Akin stood. His voice echoed and faded. "Kanoa, all we want is a little more, a little more, a little more."

I lurched from the floor of my apartment, checked my chest then walked to the bathroom and looked in the mirror. *"What am I?"*

I went to the office and balanced the sunrise in the V of my bare feet. I wasn't okay, I kept thinking of kumu, and coffee, then I picked up the package.

Part Three: Paddle In

"It's time, isn't it, Malu?" I ripped the paper off and smiled at my backpack. I opened the flap, and as I pulled out my sandals and the stickman blanket, a letter fell onto the desk.

> Dear Kanoa,
>
> In the tradition of Hawaiian kings, families select the royal wives. You must know that Kala is of ali'i, royal descent, and is to be your wife and the queen of Tronahu. This she does not know. The gods made this blanket and another for Kala when you were born. The spirit living within the blankets protected you and Kala the day of the great storm.
>
> Become the wave,
> Malu

I slipped the sandals on and placed a copy of the letter under my work shoes on Leah's desk then drove back to my house and crammed the backpack with all I needed.

After a tourist helicopter left me on Tronahu the next afternoon, I hiked to Malu's and knocked. An old woman squinted through the screen door.

Chapter 21: Home

"Is Malu here?" I asked.

She stared.

"Malu or Kiana?" I asked.

"One minute." She returned with a man in his seventies leaning on a cane.

"Can I help you?" he asked.

"Yes, I'm looking for Malu or Kiana."

The man opened the door and shuffled onto the porch. "How do you know Malu?"

"I'm Doctor Foster. I was just here, I stayed in the house next door." I pointed then stepped off the porch. The guesthouse was a roofless wooden skeleton wrapped in vines.

"What happened to the house?" I asked.

"It was destroyed in the storm many years ago."

"That's impossible." I threw out my hands. "I mean, I just slept there. Kiana fed me breakfast. Malu took me to the cove."

"You say you're a doctor?"

"Yes, but that's not why I'm here."

"Malu was my brother."

"What do you mean, *was?*"

"You don't know?"

"I don't know what?" Something was coming.

"Malu and Kiana have been gone a long time, Doctor," he said. "They died in a plane crash returning to the island on the day of the great storm."

"Died?" I stood there blinking. "What?"

"I am sorry. Are you all right?"

Part Three: Paddle In

"No, no, that's okay. I mean, I'm all right." But I wasn't. I saw a faded Volkswagen van in the driveway.

"Is that yours?" I asked.

"Yes."

"Does it run?"

"Most of the time."

"Can you give me a ride into Ohana?"

"Are you really a doctor?" he asked. "You don't look like one."

"Wait." I opened my wallet and flashed my driver's license and medical I.D.

"I will give you the keys" he said. "Just promise to bring it back."

"I promise."

The bus kicked twice, then purred, and I drove toward town. "This doesn't make sense." I pulled into the Ohana Café near dark and waited until I saw Kala serving customers. "At least she's real."

What now? Forty minutes later I was standing next to Malu's log staring at the flickering cave entrance. I should have known.

I crawled into the cavern and saw Malu's back wrapped in the yellow cloak and wearing the helmet I had seen in my dream.

"Malu, what's going on? I met your brother. He said you were killed in the storm." He didn't answer.

Chapter 21: Home

I walked around the fire and saw a circle of black amulets in front of the stickman, so I took the cue and sat down. Malu's face was painted, and he wore a shark-tooth necklace. As he pushed his palms toward the fire, the flames spiraled and dissolved the dome. At first I saw stars, then I heard voices, no — chimes — then the amber vapor I'd seen in my dream flowed through the hole and filled the cave. I looked at Malu; he was waiting. Then pumpkin-sized globes floated in and hovered above us. I smelled incense, I couldn't feel my heart, I wasn't breathing, I was floating inches above the floor.

This has to be a dream.

"You are compassion, Kanoa."

I looked through the flame into Malu's blue eyes; he gazed toward the globes then back at me, and I saw a face.

"Ken," I whispered.

Then his hair grew, and as it touched his shoulders, it turned dark with gray streaks, and his face softened into Kiana's features. Her eyes sparked then spread like a current to both orbs, her hair longer, silver, her face lined with love.

"Tutu."

As she reached toward me I saw a tattoo on her right arm; then she dropped into the he'e stance, and her form thinned and glowed. Her hair stood like lightning and broke into ten gold stars swirling above the crouching Stickman. The creature twisted toward me, and, as it stood, its chest widened as it transformed itself into the large man from my nightmares. Then the globes

Part Three: Paddle In

descended, each holding the living image of my true family, the Tronahu kings.

"Grandfather," I said. "It was you."

The large man cocked his head and nodded. "I have been with you since the day you were born, grandson. *I was the voice in your onshore breeze, the call you ignored for too long.*"

I realized what I was experiencing at that very moment was beyond time and fear and want. I knew what I was and what I needed to bring to the world. I understood that the living energy and mystery of the perfect wave I had been seeking on my surfer's journey was waiting in the potential hidden behind the societal mask that no longer fit.

"Now stand," he said. He stepped through the fire and draped the god's ancient cape of lemon yellow O'o feathers around my shoulders and placed the helmet on my head. "Kanoa, you have proven yourself by overcoming the trials and riding the great wave. Now it is time to take your rightful place as King of Tronahu, leader of the people and teacher of the principles of he'e nalu. I am proud of you. We are one." He hugged me and kissed my forehead.

"Now go," he said. "Your people are waiting."

In an orange flash, the cavern was empty except for the fire and the journal. I heard thumping outside and pulled the robe to my chest, then eased through the opening and stood on the ledge. The cove was florescent, and its shores were alive with drumbeats and torches that lit a thousand islanders while hundreds more marched like fireflies in the distance. A finger

Chapter 21: Home

of light from a full-moon touched the he'e symbol where my princess stood adorned in white. I climbed down to Kala and moved the flower to her left ear.

"I am here to save you," she said.

I knelt and kissed the palm of her right hand then stood, and we faced the people and raised our locked fingers to the gods. *"Ku'oko'a he'e nalu,"* I yelled. *"We are free to surf."*

Home

EPILOGUE

The wind romped down the volcano and tickled the koa leaves, then became a draft carrying the scent of plumeria through the attic window to become the breath of the baby prince. The aroma dipped to the lawn and skirted the cliff where it joined the offshore breeze holding the V-shaped breakers for the surfers in the cove. Kala rocked the baby wrapped in the blanket and watched the birth of another perfect morning.

"Kala, you will be late."

"Coming right now." She tucked the newborn into the bassinet and set it rocking, then flew down the stairs, kissed her mother, and scurried across the porch to the white Volkswagen bus. The grandmother tiptoed to the nursery and watched the van disappear down the hill. Ten minutes later, the mini-bus rattled into the welcome center where I was waiting in red and blue board shorts.

"I was getting a little worried," I said. I pulled Kala to my chest, and brushed my cheek against hers. "How's Malu?"

"He's doing fine. He was asleep when I left," she said. She giggled and pushed me away. "We've got a lot to do, Doctor."

"I'll get the crew to load the van," I said. "Vaccinations at both outreach clinics today, and the guests will be here at eleven o'clock." I checked my watch. "I'm going to hit some waves for an hour and I'll be back."

"Watch out for the squids."

"Not funny." I grabbed my board and hiked past the trails leading to the cottages and stopped at the beach. To my left, fishermen repaired nets strung between wooden boats, their sharp red, yellow, and blue hulls set high on logs. I sprinted along the water's edge to the sacred rock and helped the islanders place gifts over the stickman etching. The people watched, and when I raised my hands, they raised theirs, and when I was sure Kane heard my vision, I threw the board over the coral then dove into the turquoise and paddled past the third rock. The surfers parted, and I took my usual place in the line-up. I flicked my right thumb and little finger over my head and my friends returned the sign.

"King Kanoa, how did you learn to surf so well?" asked a brown-eyed boy struggling to sit on a homemade board while his father held the tail.

I squinted at the black opening in the cliff and said, "My grandfather taught me, just like your papa is teaching you."

That night, guests ambled to a bonfire that lit the façade of the cliff and outlined the cave. As instructed, they took their places on mats facing the cove; the evening sky was a moonless bowl of shooting stars. The new students were quiet and still. I approached from the dark and faced them, wearing a shark-tooth necklace, with waves painted on my face. The flames accented the yellow in my cape.

Epilogue

"Aloha. My name is Kanoa. I am King of the island of Tronahu, as were my grandfather and my ancestors.

"The forces that pulled you across the Pacific Ocean are not definable in the world you have known. By coming here, you have crossed a threshold into an unknown spiritual and mythical realm, and tonight, you will begin a passage of transformation. On this journey you will learn through experience the sacred principles and rituals taught by the gods through the sport of kings, he'e nalu."

REFERENCES

Abrams, J., & Zweig, C. (1991). *Meeting the shadow: The hidden power of the dark side of human nature.* New York: Penguin Group (USA) Inc.

Airas, E. (2014, January 6). *United States Life Tables 2009.* Retrieved October 23, 2014, from National Vital Statistics Report: http://www.cdc.gov/nchs/data/nvsr/nvsr62/nvsr62_07.pdf

Avolio, B. J., & Bass, B. M. (2004). *Multifactor leadership questionnaire: Third edition and sample set* (3rd Edition ed.). Menlo Park: Mind Garden, Inc.

Bargh, J. A. (2014, January). The unconscious mind. *Scientific American*, pp. 30–37.

Bass, B. M. (1985). *Leadership and performance beyond expectations.* New York: Free Press.

Bass, B. M., & Avolio, B. J. (1997). *Revised manual for the multifactor leadership questionnaire.* Palo Alto: Mind Garden.

Bass, B. M., & Riggio, R. E. (2006). *Transformational leadership.* New York: Psychology Press.

Beckwith, M. W. (2008). *Hawaiian mythology.* Charleston: Bibliobazaar.

Bennett, W. J. (1993). *The book of virtues.* New York: Simon and Sheuster.

Bennis, W. (2009). *On becoming a leader*. New York: Basic Books.

Bloom, H. (2009). *Blooms literary themes: The hero's journey*. (B. Hobby, Ed.) New York: Blooms Literary Criticism.

Boyatzis, R., Goleman, D., & McKee, A. (2002). *Primal leadership*. Boston: Harvard Business School Press.

Brown, B. (Director). (1966). *The Endless Summer* [Motion Picture].

Buck, P. H. (1957). *Arts and crafts of Hawaii; Clothing* (Museum Special Publication 45 ed.). Honolulu: Bishop Museum Press.

Bunson, M. R. (2002). *Encyclopedia of ancient Egypt*. Retrieved May 15, 2014, from http://www.e-reading.ws/bookreader.php/142072/Encyclopedia_of_ancient_Egypt.pdf

Burns, J. M. (1978). *Leadership*. New York: Harper & Rowe.

——— (2003). *Transforming leadership*. New York: Grove Press.

Campbell, J. (2003). *Joseph Campbell: The hero's journey Joseph Campbell on his life and work*. Novato: New World Library.

——— (1972). *Myths to live by: How to recreate ancient legends in our daily lives to release human potential*. New York: Penquin Group.

——— (2004). *Pathways to bliss: Mythology and personal transformation*. Novato: New World Library.

——— (2008). *The hero with a thousand faces* (3rd Edition ed.). Novato: New World Library.

Campbell, J., & Moyers, B. (1988). *The power of myth*. New York: Anchor Books.

Campbell, J., & Robinson, J. M. (2005). *A skeleton key to Finnigans Wake: Unlocking James Joyce's masterwork*. Navato: New World Library.

References

Carlin, F. (2009, March 26). The pursuit of happiness. *Psychology Today*, pp. 61–71.

Casey, S. (2010). *The wave: In pursuit of the rogues, freaks, and giants of the ocean*. New York: Doubleday.

Csikszentmihalyi, M. (1990). *Flow: The psychology of optimal experience*. New York: Harper Collins.

Cialdini, R. B. (2007). *The psychology of influence*. New York: HarperCollins.

Clark, J. R. (2011). *Hawaiian surfing*. Honolulu: University of Hawai'i Press.

Cook, K. R. (2011). *Kahiki: Native hawaiian relationships with other pacific islanders (Doctoral dissertation)*. Retrieved May 27, 2014, from http://deepblue.lib.umich.edu/bitstream/handle/2027.42/84558/kealanic_1.pdf?sequence=1

Dickman, M. H., & Stanford-Blair, N. (2009). *Mindful leadership: A brain based framework*. Thousand Oaks: Corwin Press.

Diodge, N. (2007). *The brain that changes itself: Stories of personal transformation from the frontiers of brain science*. Penguin Books.

Dweck, C. (2006). *Mindset: The new psychology of success*. New York: Random House, Inc.

Female hawaiian names. (1999). *20,000 Names from around the world*. Retrieved May 29, 2014, from http://www.20000-names.com/female_hawaiian_names.htm

Finney, J., & Houston, J. D. (1996). *Surfing: a history of the ancient Hawaiian sport*. San Francisco: Pomegranate Artworks.

Fornander, A. (2013). *Fornander's ancient history of the Hawaiian people* (5th Edition ed.). Honolulu: Mutual Publishing.

Frankl, V. E. (2006). *Man's search for meaning*. Boston: Beacon Press.

Freud, S. (2010). *The interpretation of dreams: The complete and definitive text*. Philadelphia: Basic Books.

Goldsmith, M., Greenberg, C. L., Robertson, A., & Hu-Cham, M. (2003). *Global leadership: The next generation*. Upper Saddle River: Prentice Hall.

Goleman, D. (1995). *Emotional intelligence: Why it can matter more than IQ*. New York: Bantam Books.

——— (2013). *Focus: The hidden driver of excellence*. New York: Harper-Collins.

Goodstein, L. D., Nolan, T. D., & Pfeiffer, J. W. (1992). *Applied strategic planning: How to develop a plan that really works*. New York: McGraw-Hill.

Grandparents. (2014). *Grandparents: Hawaiian name for grandmother*. Retrieved June 3, 2014, from About.com: http://grandparents.com.about.com/od/Grandmother-Names/g/Hawaiian-Names-For-Grandmother.htm

Halpern, C. (2008). *Making waves and riding the currents: Activism and the practice of wisdom*. San Francisco: Berrett-Koehler Publishers, Inc.

Hamilton, E. (1969). *Mythology*. New York: Back Bay Books.

Hamilton, L. (2008). *Force of nature: Mind, body, soul, and of course, surfing*. New York: Rodale.

Hawaiian dictionary. (nd). Retrieved March 9, 2015, from Internet Island: http://hawaiiandictionary.hisurf.com/dictionary-results.lasso

Hawaiian first names. (2014). *Hawaiian words; listen to the spoken word*. Retrieved May 29, 2014, from http://hawaiian-words.com/home/hawaiian-first-names/

References

Hazzard, W. R., Bierman, E. D., Blass, J. P., Ettinger, W. H., and Halter, J. B. (1994). *Principles of geriatric medicine and gerontology* (3rd Edition ed.). New York: McGraw-Hill, Inc.

Hill, C. W. L., & Jones, G. R. (2001). *Strategic management.* New York: Houghton Mifflin.

Joyce, J. (1999). *Finnigans wake.* New York: Penguin Books.

Jung, C. G. (1980). *Archtypes and the collective unconcious.* Princeton: Princeton University Press.

―――― (1974). *Dreams.* Princeton: Princeton University Press.

―――― (1964). *Man and his symbols.* London: Dell Publishing.

―――― (2010). *The undiscovered self.* Princeton: Princeton University Press.

Kahneman, D. (2011). *Thinking fast and slow.* New York: Farrar, Straus, and Giroux.

Kalakaua, D. (1990). *The legends and myths of Hawai'i: The fables and folk-lore of a strange people.* Honolulu: Mutual Publishing.

Kirch, P. V. (2010). *How chiefs became kings: Divine kingship and the rise of archaic states in ancient Hawaii.* London: University of California Press, LTD.

Kirchhoff, P. (1966). *The principles of clanship in human society.* Indianapolis: Bobbs-Merrill.

Kouzes, J. M., & Posner, B. Z. (2011). *Credibility: How leaders gain and lose it, why people demand it.* San Francisco: Jossey-Bass.

―――― (2002). *The leadership challenge.* San Francisco: Jossey-Bass.

―――― (2010). *The truth about leadership: The no-fads heart-of-the-matter facts you need to know.* San Francisco: Jossey-Bass.

Kraemer, H. M. (2011). *From values to action: The four principles of value based leadership*. San Francisco: Jossey-Bass.

Lehrer, J. (2009). *How we decide*. New York: Houghton Mifflin Harcourt.

London, J. (2012, September 18). *The joys of surfriding: How I mastered a splended sport*. Retrieved August 21, 2014, from http://theesotericcuriosa.blogspot.com/2012/09/surfing-royal-sport-as-described-by.html

Malo, D. (2010). Hawaiian antiquities. *Bernice P. Bishop Museum Special Edition Publication 2*.

Mark, J. (2013, January 17). *Egyptian Mythology*. Retrieved May 15, 2014, from http://www.ancient.eu.com/Egyptian_Mythology/

Martin, N. (2008). *Habit: The 95% of behavior marketers ignore*. Upper Saddle River: FT Press.

Merriam-Webster. (2015). http://www.merriam-webster.com/dictionary/

Moore, M. S. (2010). *Sweetness and blood: How surfing spread from Hawaii and California to the rest of the world with some unexpected results*. New York: Radale, Inc.

Motil, G. (2007). *Surfboards*. Guilford: Morris Book Publishing, LLC.

Mythology. (2014). *Ancient history encyclopedia*. Retrieved May 15, 2014, from http://ancient.eu.com/mythology/

Nolan, T. M., Goodstein, L. D. & Goodstein L. (2008). *Applied strategic planning: An introduction*. San Francisco: Pfeiffer.

Palmer, J. P. (1990). *The active life: A spirituality of work, creativity, and caring*. San Francisco: Jossey-Bass.

Pink, D. H. (2009). *Drive: The surprising truth about what motivates us.* New York: Riverhead Books.

Pinker, S. (2009). The riddle of knowing you're here. In *Time, Your brain: A user's guide* (pp. 12–19). New York: TIME Books, Time Inc.

Ramachandran, V. S. (2011). *The tell-tale brain: A neuroscientist's quest for what makes us human.* New York: W. W. Norton & Company.

Ricard, M., Lutz, A., & Davidson, R. J. (November, 2014). Mind of the meditator. *Scientific American*, pp. 39–45.

Rokeach, M. (1973). *The nature of human values.* New York: The Free Press.

Rowe, W. G., & Guerrero, L. (2011). *Cases in leadership* (2nd ed.). Los Angeles: Sage.

Samuels, M. E., Stoskopf, C. H., & Xirasagar, S. (2004). Physician leadership styles and effectiveness: An empirical study. *Medial Care Research and Review, 63* (6), 1–21.

Scharmer, C. O. (2009). *Theory U: Leading from the future as it emerges; The social technology of presencing.* San Francisco: Barrett-Koehler Publishers, Inc.

Senge, P. M. (1990). *The fifth discipline: The art and practice of the learning organization.* New York: Currency Doubleday.

Silver, N. (2012). *The signal and the noise: Why so many predictions fail — but some don't.* New York: The Penquin Press.

Snyder, R. (2001). *Fit to surf: The surfer's guide to strength training and conditioning.* Santa Cruz: Emerson Publishing Company.

Soloman, P. (Director). (2011). *Finding Joe* [Motion Picture]. Hillsboro: Beyond Words Publishing.

Spreier, S. W., Fontaine, M. H., & Malloy, R. L. (2006, June). *Leadership run amok: The destructive potential of overachievers.* Retrieved November 14, 2014, from http://www.haygroup.com/Downloads/sg/misc/Leadership_Run_Amok.pdf

Steiner, G. A. (1979). *Strategic planning: What every manager must know.* New York: The Free Press.

Thrum, T. G. (1895). Hawaiian surf riding. *Hawaiian almanac and manual for 1896*, p. 108.

Van Wart, M. (2010). Public sector leadership theory: An assessment. In J. L. Perry (Ed.), *The jossey-bass reader on nonprofit and public leadership* (pp. 73–107). San Francisco: Jossey-Bass.

Vogler, C. (2007). *The writer's journey: Mythic structure for writers.* Studio City: Michael Weise Productions.

Walter, R. (Director). (2011). *Joseph Campbell: Mythos the complete series* [Motion Picture].

Warshaw, M. (2003). *Encyclopedia of surfing.* Orlando: Harcourt, Inc.

——— (1997). *Surfriders: In search of the perfect wave.* Del Mar: Collins Publishers.

——— (2010). *The history of surfing.* San Francisco: Chronicle Books LLC.

Whitcomb, D. (2012, May 11). *Big wave surfer enters record books by riding 78 foot "monster."* Retrieved October 6, 2014, from Reuters.com: http://www.reuters.com/article/2012/05/12/us-usa-surfing-record-idUSBRE84B00120120512

Williamson, M. (1992). *A return to love: Reflections on the principles of a course in miracles.* New York: HarperCollins.

Yukl, G. (2010). *Leadership in organizations* (7th ed.). Upper Saddle River, New Jersey: Prentice Hall.

GLOSSARY OF TERMS

- *Aha alii* — a council of Hawaiian chiefs.
- *Allegory* — a story in which the characters, events, actions are symbolic and stand for truths, generalizations, and ideas about human existence, conduct, or experience.
- *Alii* — a Hawaiian chief, chiefess, ruler.
- *Alii nui* — a king; Great chief; highest ranked chief in a Hawaiian polity.
- *Archetype* — an original inherited idea, pattern, or mode of thought derived from the experience of the race and present in the unconscious of the individual.
- *Aumakua* — a spirit/deity of deceased ancestor; guardian god of the family.
- *Axis mundi* — the turning point of the world; a line through the earth's center around which the earth revolves.
- *Coydogg* — Dr. Kennedy's surfing nickname derived from Coydog, meaning a purpose-driven hybrid.
- *Hale naua* — a formal court of inquiry into the genealogies of chiefly lines at the time of the ascension of a new king.
- *He'e* — to surf or to slide.
- *He'e nalu* — to surf or slide.
- *Huaka'i* — a journey.

- *Individuation* — the process by which the self is formed by integrating the components of the conscious and the unconscious.
- *Kala* — a noble lady; princess.
- *Kanaloa* — one of the four major gods; god of the squid; god of evil.
- *Kane* — the Hawaiian creator god; a husband or the name of a godhead.
- *Kahuna* — a priest.
- *Kanoa* — the free one.
- *Kiana* — divine; heavenly.
- *Koa* — a type of Hawaiian wood used for making surfboards.
- *Ku* — an expression of the male generating parent of fertility; ancestral gods (Hine) of heaven and earth with control over fruitfulness of the earth and mankind; sun at rising is referred as Ku, at its setting Hina; god of war.
- *Ku auhau* — a specialist in the royal court responsible for maintaining and memorizing the genealogies and oral traditions of the elite (Alii).
- *Kumu* — a red Hawaiian fish.
- *Ku-oko'a* — freedom.
- *Lei niho palaoa* — a highly styled neck ornament and hook-shaped pendant carved of human hair.
- *Mana* — life force that powered the universe; supernatural or divine power.
- *Malu* — a shelter; protection; peace.

- *Mele* — a historical chant or song.
- *Metaphor* — a figure of speech or work literally denoting one kind of object or idea is used in place of another to suggest a likeness or analogy; an idea used as a symbol for something else.
- *Myth* — a vivid story or fairytale told for entertainment or to teach or explain a culture's attitude toward life, death, and the universe around it; a vehicle of communication between the subconscious and conscious.
- *Moi* — a king; sovereign.
- *Nalu* — a wave; surf.
- *Olo* — an ancient long, thick, finless surfboard made from local wood.
- *Papa he'enalu* — a surfboard.
- *Shadow* — that unconscous part of the personality that has been repressed; the "dark" part of the personality holding inferiorities, good and bad qualities, and attributes we refuse to own.
- *Tutu* — the common Hawaiian name for grandmother.

THE TEN PRINCIPLES OF HE'E NALU

1. You must seek mentors
2. You must prepare your mind, body, and soul
3. You must swim to the rocks
4. You must see your dream wave
5. You must build your own surfboard
6. You must paddle past the whitewater
7. You must defeat evil
8. You must have focus and deal with crises
9. You must go to the volcano
10. You must become the wave

CREATORS
A Business View by Dave Lakhani

Today is March 15, 2016. It is 1:32 a.m.

I can hear my daughter turning in her bed; she just turned twelve six days ago. I wonder where the next twelve years will take her. She's one of the reasons I connected with Dr. Kennedy in the first place; he knows something about kids, especially daughters.

It's funny how a daughter would bring me to a mentor right when I needed him. And how, occasionally, the tables would turn, and he could easily accept me as mentor to him.

I realize I still have a few lessons to learn.

In exactly twenty-seven hours and thirty-one minutes, I'll be fifty-one years old.

I think back . . . "When did I become an Entrepreneur?" Was it when I was eight and saw the ad in the back of a comic book that said I could sell the Grit newspaper? Or when I was eleven, riding my bike to Richard Dailey's house, my first mentor, to load up farrier equipment so I could learn how to shoe horses? Maybe it was when I was thirteen, working with the most significant mentor of my young life, Shawn Lee, who treated me like an adult, expected me to work like an adult, and stood by me when I acted like one to real adults.

I'm sure of one thing: I don't remember the first time I heard it, but as long as I can remember it was always there, a distant but distinct whisper that wouldn't go unheard, pulling me to the edge of the safety of the light, assuring me there was something more. Compelling me.

"You have to do this. Nothing else will be enough, the reward is worth the risk."

I'm confident that, at some moment, every creator has the same experience, but especially Entrepreneurs — creators of businesses, big ideas, and brilliant people.

Most people won't listen. They'll settle for less, for mediocrity, they'll stay comfortably in their ordinary world. At the end of their lives, in every study, people don't regret the things they did, they regret the things they didn't do, the calls to adventure they didn't answer.

Entrepreneurs, Leaders, and Creators can't sit back and do nothing; they can't ignore the call to adventure. It's simply not possible.

When you hear the call and you start on your journey, *The Surfer's Journey* will be your first guide.

The Surfer's Journey tale unfolded on many levels for me. While many will see this book as a guide to a personal, transformational journey to find their own bliss, I see it as a universal story of the Creator, who not only finds his or her own bliss but brings the elixir back to their team, their tribe, their followers and fans. They help them find their bliss, too (and that is the real secret of what makes the hero heroic).

Rather than selfishly keeping their newfound knowledge to themselves, they realize the importance of sharing the elixir with all who will receive it. They willingly set them on their own journeys with a set of lessons, hard won, to evolve, build on, and return to when they become the mentor.

While taking on *The Surfer's Journey*, you'll discover the leader of the self, the family, the business, the community, the nation, and the world. Done properly, leadership is less about the leader than it is about the preparation of the follower to blaze his or her own trail.

In business we hear and use the word "empowerment" a lot. True empowerment isn't giving the employee the ability to make a decision to do what is right for a customer. True empowerment is giving the employee the foundational lessons to grow so that they know intuitively what to do for the customer and when, because it is what you yourself would do.

You are the key to them getting to that destination faster, easier, and more predictably than if they'd tried to create a path on their own without direction or helpful allies. Mentors empower people to be their best selves in every situation and to act courageously. Managers empower people to do a certain set of things within a narrow range of limits to avoid mistakes. Mentors understand that real mastery comes through failure than through success.

Who are you being with your team today? Who does your team need you to be? There are a thousand lessons in this short book but only one hero, one leader.

It's you.

You'll be surprised when you see yourself and surprised at where the mentor will take you. You'll also be surprised where you end up leading your business.

I've been fortunate enough to have Dr. Kennedy as a literal mentor in some key areas and times during my life. I have to say, I'm a little irritated that he held back some of the lessons for this book . . . or did he just know I wasn't ready for them yet?

Your adventure won't be he same as mine, but our destinations are the same. The lessons of *The Surfer's Journey* will get us both there with fewer struggles.

As you progress through the surfer's journey in this book, you'll discover the ten principles of HE'E NALU.

Walk through each of the lessons once, then again. But the next time, look at them not only through the lens of the Entrepreneur and Creator, but also Parent, Partner, Spouse, Community Leader, and every other role you play.

Do you notice how the Surfer's (Hero's) Journey applies to every area and how it is a predictable model you can follow to create success in every area of your life or business?

In reality, Creators do more than create one thing. The most successful Creators realize that they are creating more than art or a business; they are creating families, communities, countries, nations, and a world. And without you and I, none of it would exist. You can't create or lead a business, family, community or tribe without first completing your own journey. You are already on your heroic journey now with Dr. Kennedy as your trusted mentor for this part of the trip.

It's your time. Dig deep, paddle hard, pop up and get into position. Your wave is here! The world is waiting — for you. And what ONLY YOU can create!

—Dave Lakhani
Journeyer, Creator, Partner, Father,
Mentor, and now, Blissful Surfer!
CEO Bold Approach, Inc.
Author of *Persuasion: The Art of Getting What You Want*
and *Power of an Hour*

ABOUT DR. KENNEDY

Dr. Don Kennedy is a respected authority in the research and teaching of leadership and motivation. He is a family and urgent care physician, author, professional speaker, business consultant, adjunct medical and college professor, and has surfed for over sixty years.

The author is a diplomat of the American College of Family Medicine, holds a PhD in Leadership, Masters in Business Administration, and is a member of the American Association for Physician Leadership and National Speakers Association. He has spoken for companies including Young Life, Rotary International, The American Association for Physician Leadership, and is involved with Narcotics Anonymous.

Dr. Kennedy created and practices motivational medicine and teaches leadership and health and wellness through *The Surfer's Journey* seminars, private client mentoring and coaching, and university-based courses.

Other books include the internationally published *5 A.M. & Already Behind* with forward by bestselling author Michael Gerber and *Your Smoking Bahbit: 7 Steps to Stop Smoking Now.*

Raised in poverty as the son of a professional bull rider and single waitress, Dr. Kennedy's surfer's journey is a remarkable testimonial to the willpower of personal vision and survival. He has been married for over thirty years, is the father of four, grandfather of three, and is the founder and CEO of *The Surfer's Journey, LLC* and co-founder of the *Mind, Body and Soul Surfing Club*. He still surfs!

> **Please Join Dr. Kennedy's Email List at:**
> *http://www.drdonkennedy.com*

Coming Soon: The Surfer's Journey Podcast

IT'S TIME TO PADDLE OUT!
How to Begin Your Surfer's Journey

It would be easy to let you think this is the end of the book and that you would be left alone to fend off the monsters that are waiting to stop your surfer's journey, but that's not going to happen. Remember, I wrote this fable to teach people stuck on the *beach of same* how to get past the whitewater and become the transformational hero and leader the people who need them are waiting for. That person is you!

Just as I have told my patients for thirty years and just as Malu said to Kanoa, "I am here to carry you beyond the threshold of the meaningless." That means you need to know that I will never give up on you; we are paddling out together.

That said, I thought it would be fun to have Malu mentor you, so we have set up *Malu-grams* to help to motivate, inspire and challenge the surfer in you to listen to that voice that keeps calling you to discover what you are. It's time to go to the link below to begin your walk along the cove; *Malu is waiting for you.*

http://www.drdonkennedy.com/malu-grams

What Are You?

For information on motivational medicine,
teaching, mentoring, Surfer's Journey seminars and
other books, please go to my personal website:

http://www.drdonkennedy.com

www.ingramcontent.com/pod-product-compliance
Lightning Source LLC
Chambersburg PA
CBHW070605300426
44113CB00010B/1414